Kingdom Builders

Assembling God's Divine
Design Here on Earth

Prophetic Courier

Dedication

This book is dedicated to the body of Christ. Dear kingdom builders, the time has come! The Lord has need of every one of us. United, we arise. United, we build. United, we stand! Manifested unity in Jesus' name.

"For I know the thoughts that I think toward you, saith the Lord, 'Thoughts of peace, and not of evil, to give you an expected end'" (Jeremiah 29:11, KJV).

"Wherein He hath abounded toward us in all wisdom and prudence; having made known unto us the mystery of His will, according to His good pleasure which He hath purposed in Himself: that in the dispensation of the fulness of times He might gather together in one all things in Christ, both which are in heaven, and which are on earth; even in Him" (Ephesians 1:8-10, KJV).

Acknowledgments

I would like to thank the Lord for my Word Alive Outreach Ministries family in Augusta, Georgia, and my Turning Point Church family in Corpus Christi, Texas, for teaching the unadulterated truth of the Gospel of Jesus Christ and always demonstrating God's agape love. I want to thank the Lord for my personal Trilogy publishing team, who diligently worked with me during the final process of birthing this book. Special thanks are going out to every individual who faithfully labored with me in prayer and encouraged me to keep pushing when I felt like quitting. Above all, I thank my heavenly Father for choosing me to deliver His heavenly mail to the body of Christ at this *appointed time*. I am forever grateful.

Table of Contents

Foreword

"The author shares throughout this book her vivid testimony comparing God's divine design like a jigsaw puzzle or a construction site. This book inspired by God Himself will give you deep-detailed revelation, insight, and understanding for your life. Simply a revelatory tool that will lead you in the right direction and answer questions you may have been asking God in your prayer time. This book will build you up so you can walk in your God's divine design for your life. 'See, I have this day set you over the nations and over the kingdoms, to root out and to pull down, to destroy and to throw down, to build up and to plant' (Jeremiah 1:10, NIV)."

—Prophetess Bella A. Davis
Heart to Heart Healing Ministries
Founder/Overseer

Preface

Growing up in the Word of the Lord, I had to learn to be sensitive to His voice and obey Him, no matter what it cost me. In my youth, I was misunderstood. Many called me foolish and simple-minded. At the time, I thought it was an insult, and I used to cry. Today, I am still misunderstood. Occasionally, I am still called simple-minded and foolish. However, today I accept those words as compliments. Now, I understand that God takes the foolish things of the world to put to shame the wise.

> *It is written*: "But God chose the foolish things of the world to shame the wise; God chose the weak things of the world to shame the strong. God chose the lowly things of this world and the despised things—and the things that are not—to nullify the things that are, so that no one may boast before Him" (1 Corinthians 1:27-29, NIV).

God has always used the simplest things to speak His mysteries to me. Before revealing what He wants me to see, He always says, "First natural, then spiritual."

> *It is written:* "The spiritual did not come first, but the natural, and after that the spiritual" (1 Corinthians 15:46, NIV).

It is simple things such as a jigsaw puzzle and construction sites that He demonstrated with power how to effectively kingdom build while we are in this world. God has a *Divine Design*, a plan already in place for us. He already knows our end from our beginning.

> *It is written:* "Declaring the end from the beginning, and from ancient times the things that are not yet done, saying, My counsel shall stand, and I will do all My pleasure" (Isaiah 46:10, KJV).

He already knows our ending. This is His story. We are characters in His book. A book writer knows how their story ends and how it starts. A book writer has the power to add on and erase. God is the Author of authors. He wrote *the* book and designed *the* divine plan. He is *the* Architect, and we are His workers/laborers...

I Am that I Am sent me at this set time to deliver His messages to the body of Christ in simplicity of what He wants us to focus on while we are on this earth. We are to be in this world and not of it. God says He wants His body back in order. He wants us to be in alignment with His divine design. The body of Christ has been dysfunctional too long. The Lord says there are too many of us claiming to be saved, but we are still basking in sin. There are too many of us straying away from His Word. There are too many lost sheep that we are being nonchalant about finding.

The Lord says, "I chose you and set you apart as Holy, but you want to keep going back to blending in with the sin. How long do you think I will keep allowing you to behave like orphan children?" The Lord is giving us space to repent, live holy, and set apart as His chosen vessels.

I Am that I Am sent me to enforce His Word and compel His people to get back in alignment with His Word and to remind us that He is coming back for a church without spot or wrinkle. If you are reading this book, there is something in it for you. God does not make mistakes. He already designed from the beginning of time that you would be reading this book at this appointed time. I pray that the life-changing word in the text be received and applied to your life. I pray that the contents in this book effectively demonstrate the Word of God with power.

I pray for every member that the Lord leads to this book will read it with an open mind and softened heart. I pray that this book opens doors for salvation, repentance, healing, and deliverance. I pray that this is a life-changing encounter for many souls from the north, south, east, and west. Above all, I pray that the Lord receive all the glory and all the praise in Jesus' name. Amen.

Introduction

In the beginning, God created everything in six days, and on the seventh day, He rested.

> *It is written*: "By the seventh day God had finished the work He had been doing; so on the seventh day He rested from all His work. Then God blessed the seventh day and made it holy, because on it He rested from all the work of creating that He had done" (Genesis 2:2-3, NIV).

He knows our end from our beginning because He already created it in the beginning! He knows the outcome of each of us and this world. God placed us here on this earth with a divine purpose.

There is so much havoc in the world today. So many of us have deviated from our *first* love. A lot of us are in panic mode. Some of us are straying away from our faith in Him. Some of us have chosen to do our own thing, which does not include Him.

Some of us have allowed fear, doubt, unbelief, and compromise in our midst to knock us out of alignment with His will. Many of us have gotten so caught up in the cares of this world to where we are following other gods. Some of us have stopped building for Him because of all the persecutions.

Five years ago, the Lord had me sit down and assemble a jigsaw puzzle so I could comprehend in clarity what it was He wanted to use me to speak to His people concerning His divine design for us. He needed my *simple mind* to reveal "some" of the mysteries of His divine design. He did not want me to go *scuba deep* when sharing the mysteries with the body of Christ. I had to obey and write in simplicity what the Lord is saying in this hour about His kingdom builders that are supposed to be building for Him.

In the process of writing this book, the Lord revealed to me the things He was not pleased with that needed to be corrected in my life. He wanted to make sure that I remained humble while delivering

His messages. I am a part of the body of Christ. Messengers are not omitted from the messages given. We are all one body with many members. When one of us falls short, it affects the whole body.

Imagine this: You stomped your baby toe, and you feel the pain. At the moment, you may scream or cry. Your whole body got upset behind that baby toe. While it was throbbing, you might have held it with your hands to try and calm the pain. You checked it out to make sure it was not bleeding, missing a toenail, or broken, and you may limp, sit down, etc.

If a hurting baby toe can affect different parts of our natural bodies, what difference is it when someone in the body of Christ is spiritually ill? *Selah!*

That one member we may think is the least in the body of Christ can cause a lot of pain to the whole body if he or she is spiritually hurt or sick. In the same way, we would nurture our physical bodies when pained; we should also nurture our spiritual bodies. Amen.

No one is omitted when the Lord is chastising His body. There are no big "I's" or little "u's" in the body of Christ. We are one. It is time to stop operating in the spirit of division and unit as one. One mind, one body, one Christ. Amen.

The intention of this book is to uproot what should not be; to plant and to water so that He alone may get the glory. We, as His kingdom builders here on this earth, need to get busy for the Lord and stop procrastinating or allowing distractions of this world to hinder us from building.

> *It is written*: "We must lay aside every weight and the sin that which doth so easily beset us" (Hebrews 12:1, KJV).

Time is winding down. He *will* be back for His church without a spot or blemish—time to arise and build. If you are already building, time to put in some overtime. He is coming back very soon. Amen.

The Jigsaw Puzzle Assignment

Obedience

I remember, as a child, I used to love spending time assembling jigsaw puzzles. As I grew older, I did not have the time or the interest in any kind of puzzle. Sometimes I would start them, but I would seldom finish them.

I was astounded when the Lord compelled me to buy a jigsaw puzzle back in October of 2016. I was at a dollar store buying some items for myself with my last six or seven dollars when I heard the Lord say, "Get that puzzle." I was hesitant to do it because I only had a few dollars, and I was too busy trying to buy what I could with that little money I had. I had picked up a candy bar and a few other things, trying to wisely stretch my money. The Lord told me to put it back and get the jigsaw puzzle. It was a specified five-hundred-piece jigsaw puzzle He ordered me to buy. I picked it up, but when I got to the register, I "slickly" put it back down while I was in the checkout line. My eyes were locked on the sweets on display at the checkout counter. I attempted to pick up a piece of candy once more. Of course, the Lord was not going to allow me to get away with buying candy after He had already instructed me to buy a jigsaw puzzle. I heard Him say again, "Put that candy back and get *that* jigsaw puzzle."

What was wrong with me? I did not want to obey God and get that jigsaw puzzle. My flesh was stinking up the place, trying to get me to submit to it and not God.

We have got to get to the point in our lives of knowing when we hear the voice of God and obey Him, even when it seems like little simple things are not harmful. The Lord will take those simple little things to use for His glory. The things we may think do not have purpose can play a big role in our lives at any time. It is vital for us to listen to His voice and obey Him. Our lives very well depend on it.

Flesh at War with the Spirit

> "For he that soweth to his flesh shall of the flesh reap corruption; but he that soweth to the Spirit shall of the Spirit reap life everlasting" (Galatians 6:8, KJV).

How many of us know that God will give us an unexpected assignment just like that? Oftentimes, we may tussle with it at the beginning, but we later submit to the assignment given. Our spirit may be willing while our flesh may fall weak. We may get up enough strength to pick that thing up for a minute, but sometimes it is turned into a forgotten memory. We might call it an impulse. It may have been something we thought about for a split second but later changed our minds. Well, sometimes that usually be the Lord telling us to do some things, and our flesh is struggling with our spirit.

The spirit of God in us wants to obey, but the flesh wants the opposite of whatever the Spirit of God in us wants. By yielding to our flesh, it will cause us to walk in error/disobedience to God. When we have a divine assignment from the Lord, the enemy will try to make us feel crazy and double-minded.

I found myself second-guessing God when I knew I heard Him tell me to buy the puzzle. I knew He was not going to just let me sit around and waste time putting together a puzzle that had no meaning behind it.

> *It is written*: "So I say, walk by the Spirit, and you will not gratify the desires of the flesh. For the flesh desires what is contrary to the Spirit, and the Spirit what is contrary to the flesh. They are in conflict with each other, so that you are not to do whatever[a] you want" (Galatians 5:16-17, NIV).

The Lord had a jigsaw puzzle waiting on me to assemble. The puzzle was full of meat; my spiritual protein was there waiting for me. My flesh wanted the sugar, but my spirit wanted the meat. How many of us know that sugars are not good for the body? How many

15

of us know that if we sow into the flesh, we reap death, but if we sow into the spirit, we reap life?

The jigsaw puzzle was a needed nutriment that helped me to see more clearly so I could grow spiritually. God wanted to demonstrate to me in simplicity through the jigsaw puzzle how the body of Christ, which includes me, is falling short with kingdom building. My flesh knew correction was coming. That is why it did not want to yield to buying the jigsaw puzzle. However, I overcame my flesh and obeyed God.

To think, if I had not obeyed Him and bought that jigsaw puzzle, if I had yielded to my fleshly desire and bought the candy bar, I would have been walking in total disobedience to Him. Furthermore, I would not have been able to write this book. I could not have just written a book of a revelation of how His divine design is like a jigsaw puzzle on my own. I could not have been able to document in detail each revealed part if I had not gone through the process of assembling a jigsaw puzzle.

I yielded to His voice and accepted His assignment with the provision (*the jigsaw puzzle*). By obeying Him, I was able to hear Him speak to me in clarity about some of His divine design mysteries. As a bonus, He compelled me to write a book about it in a simple form. He said to share what He revealed to me with my siblings in Christ and to include all my personal bloopers and blunders. He told me not to leave any of my mess out or try to sugar coat it while sharing.

It is written: "And they overcame Him by the blood of the Lamb, and by the word of their testimony; and they loved not their lives unto the death" (Revelation 12:11, NIV).

A lot of us miss the mark because we are full of the flesh. We are too busy feeding flesh what it wants. Flesh will cause us to be rebellious and not submit to Him and His Word. Flesh does not belong in heaven. Flesh was created from the dust of the ground. When it is all said and done, flesh will return to the dust of the ground.

I speak now in the name of Jesus, turn-around for everyone that might be battling with flesh when the Lord gives an assignment. Thank You, Lord, that we are not slaves to our flesh. We shall mortify the deeds of our flesh. We shall pick up our crosses daily, crucify our flesh and follow You, Lord. We yield ourselves to You, oh Lord, and Your Word every day and in every way. For Your Word is life, and it is truth. Flesh shall die as the Spirit of God arises in us. None of us, Lord, but all of You in Jesus' name. Flesh shall *not* glory in Your sight. Amen.

It is written: "Those who belong to Christ Jesus have crucified the flesh with its passions and desires" (Galatians 5:24, NIV).

"For if ye live after the flesh, ye shall die: but if ye through the Spirit do mortify the deeds of the body, ye shall live" (Romans 8:13, KJV).

"That no flesh should glory in His presence" (1 Corinthians 1:29, KJV).

Stinking Thinking

For though we walk in the flesh, we do not war after the flesh: (For the weapons of our warfare are not carnal, but mighty through God to the pulling down of strong holds;) Casting down IMAGINATIONS, and every high thing that exalteth itself against the knowledge of God, and bringing into captivity every thought to the obedience of Christ; And having in a readiness to revenge all disobedience, when your obedience is fulfilled.

2 Corinthians 10:3-6 (KJV)

Thinking back to the day I brought the jigsaw puzzle *assignment* home. I remember sitting there and looking at the box. I looked at how difficult the design appeared to be. I looked at how many pieces it came with and thought about how long it would take to put it together. My thoughts were all over the place. My stinking thinking about the assignment had kicked in. *I* decided that *I* was not about to sit down and spend *my time* piecing together a puzzle. I had too much on my plate to do already. *I* was like, nope, not today. At the time, I did not realize it, but I had an "I, me, and my" problem! I behaved as a hardheaded and rebellious child showing disrespect to my Father. I was being self-centered. Although I was doing other ministries and the Lord was using me mightily, I was still disobeying Him. I was questioning His authority. I accepted the assignment and still did not comply to it. I had the nerve to say I was not spending "my time" putting a puzzle together. My thinking was funkier than a skunk.

I knew that God told me to buy the puzzle. I knew that He had messages in the puzzle to show me. I knew that they would bless me and others, but...there it is, the Christian curse word "but." I thought I was not good enough. I was focusing on all the successful book writers. I was watching God use so many of His powerhouse people bountifully. I became scared. I thought, *Who am I?* Over and over, I said to myself, "I cannot write or speak as good as those book writers and preachers." At times, I stutter. I cannot think of all those big, sound good words to use like all those powerhouse preachers.

The more I focused on all those things, the more scared I became. Fear was closing in to completely overshadow my faith. I started to fool myself, saying it was not God who told me to buy the puzzle and document/write the revelations. It could not have been Him. God knows I cannot do that. I thought I was going to stay in my comfort zone. Instead of bringing into captivity every negative thought that did not line up with the Word of God, I was entertaining them. So, I allowed my mind battles to defeat me.

The jigsaw puzzle I brought home that day ended up on my coffee table. It later ended up in my room on the dresser. Then it went from the room dresser back to my living room in the drawer of my television stand. Before I knew it, almost two months had passed, and the puzzle still had not been assembled. It had been put away in a drawer and forgotten about. I allowed my thoughts to shift me away from the divine plan. Please do not judge me. Truth be told, I am sure that we all have gone through similar struggles with different situations.

One day in the month of December, I was looking for something (I cannot remember what), and I opened the drawer and saw the puzzle. Immediately, I felt a tugging in my spirit to pull the puzzle out and work on it. When I pulled it out of the drawer and looked at the picture on the box, I was feeling some type of way all over again about assembling the puzzle. However, as I said before, my desire was to do the will of the Lord. It does not matter how much I struggled then or now; I choose to obey Him. I refused to be defeated once more by my own mind. I chose to shut those thoughts down and meditate on God's Word.

Any thoughts that do not line up with His Word do not come from Him. We should immediately kick them out when they attempt to enter. It is imperative to protect our minds from impure thinking. Every day we should put on our whole armor of God and especially make sure that we put on our helmet of salvation. We should think about what His Word says about us. At times demons will use others to say things to us that are not true just to have us thinking about it.

In the name of Jesus, let us uproot every seed that was sown in our minds that does not line up with the Word of God. Let us call a crop failure to the harvest now in the name of Jesus. Every stinking thought is bound, cast out, and down in the name of Jesus. The Lord says He knows the thoughts that He has for us are good and not evil. We shall accept and realign our thinking to His divine design in Jesus' name. We are who God says we are, and we can do what God says we can do. God counted us worthy. He anointed, appointed, and approved us from the foundations of the world. Anything spoken against His Word that He already designed for our lives we call null and void in Jesus' name. Lord, thank You for keeping us in perfect peace because our minds are stayed on You. Thank You, Lord, for clean, pure, positive, heavenly thoughts in the name of Jesus. Amen.

Precise Timing

"There is a time for everything, and a season for every activity under the heavens."
(Ecclesiastes 3:1, NIV)

When the Lord gives us assignments, He also gives us a set time to complete them. Most of the time, we do not know that He has given us a certain time to finish the assignment. When we think we are late, we are not. According to His time, we are on schedule. For instance, for two months, I was avoiding putting a jigsaw puzzle together and had felt bad about it when I realized how much time it took me to finally submit to the assignment. I started assembling the puzzle on the *set time* God had already planned from the beginning of time. I was right on His divine time schedule. God knows exactly what He is always doing. He is not double-minded or confused about anything.

The Lord has revealed to me how to move in His divine timing. When we line up with His divine timing, we will see more of the *supernatural* realm.

Notice how we, as the body of Christ, always want the Lord to come when we want Him to come, but we take time about doing things for Him? He already knew that, at times, we were going to be slow to obey Him. So, He was merciful and stretched His time for us to get it together. Trust that we are going to go through something in that timeframe because He must do some shifting, turning, and pruning to get us to yield to lining back up with His will.

One of the *purposes* of Him having me assemble the jigsaw puzzle was to learn how to control my flesh and thoughts when He gives assignments to me and to share with others who may be struggling with the same issue. God showed me some very ugly things about myself in that process. I am sure that my testimony of stinking thinking and funky flesh might have shined some light on some of the readers of this book. It was a sure ouch, but amen and thank You,

Lord, for having mercy on me. He could have just cut me off, but He did not. Glory to God.

How many of us know that when God gives us a vision, word, or something, sometimes it does not mean to start on it right then? He may give us a ministry and give us step-by-step instructions for putting it together, but sometimes it may not mean for us to do it all at once. In this day and time, as an example, God may tell us to go rent a building for a church. We may go out and rent the building. We may go broke trying to buy everything to get the church up and running. We may go as far as persuading members of other churches to join our ministries. We may take up two and three offerings, have church functions with charging ridiculous fees to enter, have tons of fundraisers, and so on, trying to keep the church open and running. We may do all of that when God said go get the building *only*.

The thoughts I had behind the puzzle were "stinking thinking" thoughts. When God tells us to do something, He expects us to do it precisely how and when He says to do it. God says so many of us have missed Him because we did not move when He told us to move, or we may attempt to do the extra that He did not tell us to do. We may sit around and say, "I know God told me to do this, but why did it happen like…?" Yes, God may have told us to do it, but know this, we must precisely obey Him and be in precise timing with Him, or we will miss Him.

Imagine this: You do not have the money to pay your rent, and you have gone everywhere that normally assist with rental payments, but they all turn you away, and you are still stuck with owing the rent. Your time is winding down, and you are about to get evicted. Then the Lord whispers to you to get up and go to the grocery store to buy some toilet paper. You know you need toilet paper, but you do not want to buy it because you know you need every penny to pay your rent. So, you do not move. You begin to do other things, and the Lord comes back again and tells you to go to the store. You may sit there for a while. You may take your time about going, but you know it is the Lord telling you to go to the store. After a while, you finally get up and go to the store and buy the toilet tissue and go back home. Your situation is still the same. You still need rent money, and now on top of that, the money you do have is less than it was before you went to the store to purchase the toilet tissue. Thoughts enter your mind about hearing God telling you to go to the store and buy toilet tissue. You now doubt that you heard Him tell you to go to the store and buy the tissue.

Okay, now let me use the same scenario a different way.

Imagine this: You are hurting for rent money, and everyone is turning their back on you. You are getting more "no's" than anything else from people you know that can help you. Your time is winding down, and you need a financial breakthrough. The money that you have is not enough to pay your rent, and you are standing in need of toilet tissue (something you can buy but refuse to spend any money on). The Lord tells you to get up and go to the store and buy some toilet tissue. You immediately get up and go to the store to buy toilet tissue. The store you end up going to is doing a door prize for the 10,000th customer that walks through the door will win a five-hundred-dollar shopping spree plus a thousand dollars cash to show their customers appreciation of keeping their store in business for so many odd years. They were not advertising the door prize because they knew it would attract a lot of people for the wrong reasons.

Because you obeyed God and got up and went to the store when He said go; you were the 10,000th customer, and you won the door prize. Not only did you have enough money to pay your rent, but you also won a shopping spree. How many of us know that God is a God of abundance? When He blesses us, He does it with an abundance, an overflow.

Again, I must say that God's timing is perfect. When we move on His time and be precisely obedient with it, it will cause us to tap into the supernatural realm and receive what He has already ordained for us to have from the beginning of time. His people will have a life-changing experience. All the glory *will* reflect to God Almighty. Amen.

The Source of Every Resource

If we keep going to the same sources expecting them to help us, then how is God going to get His glory? God says He is tired of us giving credit to people who do not deserve it. If the agency had paid your rent, you would have thought it was them who paid it. I know you may say, "No, I would not have; I know God is the one that used them to bless me." Well, let me back this up and shine a little light on it. If someone wanted a referral of where they could go to pay their rent, you would refer them to the agency because they paid your rent for you. Well, that is taking God's glory from Him and giving it to the agency. God wants us to come to Him. In Him, His answers are yes and amen. People may go to agencies to get temporary help, but God says if we come to Him, He will help us abundantly with an overflow. He is not a temporary Provider. The agencies do not deserve the praise; God does! When God gives us a "fish's mouth" blessing, no one will be able to take the glory from Him. No one will have to ask where it came from because we would know it had to only be Him.

If anyone ever comes to one of us for recommendations, we should refer them to the Lord instead of the natural sources. Sometimes God will give us favor with certain people and things that He will not give to others. They have their own favor. The best response is when someone asks us where or how just to lift our hands and point towards heaven and say, "God did it"! What is so hard about giving Him all the praise and glory?

God says we need to stop expecting the people and things to give us what we need. How can we expect the natural when we serve a supernatural God? Remember how Jesus told Peter to go to the water and retrieve a coin from out of a fish mouth?

It is written: "Notwithstanding, lest We should offend them, go thou to the sea, and cast an hook, and take up the fish that first cometh up; and when thou hast opened his mouth, thou shalt find a piece of money: that take, and give unto them for Me and thee" (Matthew 17:27, KJV).

Imagine with me a sea full of fish and fishermen, but there is one fish at that precise time right there waiting for Peter to come get a coin out of his mouth. Really? One would think that the fish would have been dead or dying from choking on the piece of money that was in its mouth. I can only imagine that the fish was glad to see Peter. It was glad that Peter freed it from the coin.

Prophecy: God is showing me how you, yes you, the person who is reading this book right now. God is about to give you a "fish's mouth" blessing. Stop looking for a natural way and focus on the supernatural. Listen to hear the voice of God give you instructions and be willing to move *precisely* when He says to move and watch what He release. I cannot say it enough. We serve a supernatural God.

If we move when God says to move and how He says to move, He will reveal what He has already provided for the assignment He gives us. We may hear Him and just dive right in, and then we wonder why things do not happen the way we think they should or when we think they should. Sometimes we make unnecessary messes. If God gives us the vision, He also will provide for it. Everything operates on God's time. What He ordains, He will maintain/sustain. He is the Source of every resource. Amen.

Obedience is not just the key. It is precise obedience that opens the door to abundant and overflowed blessings. We all can do something the Lord tells us to do, but if we are not doing it *exactly* when or how He tells us to do it, it is the same as disobeying. This is a season of unusual. God is blessing His people in unusual ways. He is throwing His weight all over the place. It is vital to hear Him and *precisely* obey Him. We need to move when He says move and do what He says to do *precisely* how and when He says! Amen.

Finally, with a cleared mind, I brought the puzzle to the table and decided to sincerely obey God and put the puzzle together no matter what. My Dad holds all the time in His hands. He can redeem it, hold it up, fast forward it or take it away. How many of us know that He does whatever He wants with time because He is the One who created it from the very beginning?

Time and Ministry

In ministry, we must have plenty of patience. If we are in leadership or we are more advanced than some members in the body of Christ, patience must run deep within us.

We cannot rush God while working deliverance ministry. There are some churches today that rely on a program lineup to assure that services end on *their* scheduled time. Some may go as far as altering the program services by reducing or eliminating those who were on the schedule for the sake of time. Usually, churches that focus more on time than the move of God are ineffective with healing, deliverance, and spiritual growth. We cannot expect a move from God when we try to control the church services. However, how many of us know that when God wants something done during a service, the Holy Spirit will step in and *alter* the service? Some leaders of their churches will move out of the way and allow the Lord to have His way in the service. Unfortunately, there are some leaders that will see God moving and still try to shift the service back to the regularly scheduled program. A church that will not allow the Lord to have His way because it does not fit in with their program time is completely out of alignment with the Lord.

It is written: "Quench not the Spirit" (1 Thessalonians 5:19, KJV).

It is not about us. It is all about Him. Who are we to step in His house and try to overthrow His ways? How many of us say, "As long as you are in my house, you are going to follow my rules. Is it my way or the highway"? Again, why do we think we can sit in His house and try to overthrow Him? When we move out of the way and realize that we are on God's time, not our own, and allow Him to have His way so that everything can flow according to His divine plan. Souls will be saved, healed, and delivered. And God would receive the authentic praise He deserves.

The Material/Supplies

"But my God shall supply all your need according to His riches in glory by Christ Jesus" (Philippians 4:19, KJV).

He then told me to look at the amount of puzzle pieces in the puzzle. He said, "Notice how the puzzle comes with all the pieces you need to complete the visual on the box?" He said, "For My divine design, all the pieces are already there. Just as a jigsaw puzzle, the way you find the pieces and put them together, you must do the same with the body of Christ. That is why you cannot pick and choose who you want to work with."

We confess that He supplies our every need, but sometimes we think we are missing something because things may not be going the way we think they should be going. If He supplies, then we must know that there is nothing missing. Sometimes it is us who throw away or try to build without the supplies that God has already given us. Sometimes when we behave in that manner, God will allow things to flop. Ask me how I know. There have been several times the Lord will tell us to do something, and it may fall through. That is because we were trying to use the supplies and build with them ourselves instead of working with the ones that had the knowledge of how to use the supplies. We may not want to work with certain people because of our secret hate, jealousy, personal vendettas towards one another. Some of us would rather build on our own with bitter hearts and not realizing that we are building in vain. Yes, God will allow that type of foolishness to flop.

We will not successfully build anything for Him harboring iniquity in our hearts for one another.

There are some of us who may have the finances and a team of followers willing to be a part of helping us build something for the Lord. The thing is, God may not have authorized us to build that thing. Sometimes it may be a good thing, but it is not a God thing. When we build things without God appointing or approving it, nine-point-nine times out of ten, it is a man-made ministry with the "self" centered, mammon motive type ministry. Ministries can be imitated, but the anointing of God on them cannot be duplicated.

There is someone that is reading this book that needs to hear this:

Prophecy: do not be discouraged when you see those who have the material and team to build and you do not. God already has your team and supplies ready. Remember, we all have an appointed time. When it does come, you better be ready. It will not be the time to get ready. You have already had more than enough time to prepare. Keep your eyes on Him. Move when He says to move and not a second too soon or a second too late. Stop worrying. Your time is coming. Also, before building anything, make sure you have the right motives. God is not going to approve anything that is deceptively, competitively, selfishly built. It is all about Him. He said that when He is lifted up from the earth, He will draw all men to Him, not us.

> *It is written*: "And I, when I am lifted up[a] from the earth, will draw all people to Myself" (John 12:32, NIV).

We have got to stop trying to build with the material we have not yet been trained to use. That is like having a bricklayer trying to use an electrician's conduit bender to lay his bricks. If we want to know how to use a certain tool that we do not know how to use, we must go through the learning process to become skilled in that area. There is no way around it. When we attempt to operate a tool without the knowledge could be harmful to ourselves and others.

Knowledge is a tool needed for building. We, as the body of Christ, are not supposed to hold back any kingdom knowledge from our siblings in Christ. The body of Christ has it bad in this time with holding back information that will help strengthen our siblings in Christ's ability to effectively build. Many of us would prefer to die with the knowledge before sharing it with someone else. Could it be that we do not choose to share the knowledge because we fear that person would be greater than us? Intercessors, let us pray for our siblings in Christ that are very knowledgeable about the Gospel to share it with other members of the body and without attaching outrageous fees to it. God's Word is not for sale. Amen, release, release, release in Jesus' name.

Let us also pray for those who do not want to sit under the skilled kingdom builders to learn how to be more effective builders. The body of Christ has it bad in this area as well. Instead of sitting under those who God has placed in authority and learning, some of us will leave the ministry and start our own. Sometimes that is why we see some of our siblings in Christ ministries appear to be on life support, in incubators due to premature birth, or dead. It is imperative to sit down and learn before we get up and try to lead.

Visualizing

Before opening the puzzle box, the Lord told me to look at the picture on the box. He said, "The puzzle is *always bigger* than the picture on the box." He said, "My design is *bigger* than the visions you see."

Have you ever driven by a construction site and saw a *coming soon* sign with a picture of whatever they were building? Did you take a moment out of curiosity to see what was on the picture? Like everyone else who passes a construction site, we are curious to know just what it is that is coming soon. We cannot tell while they are building what they are building. If we decide to give them our business or not, we are still curious to know what is going on at a construction site. It does not matter if it is building work or road work; we are going to look.

When we see the "after" on the picture and look over at the builders, we may not be able to see how a beautiful building will come from a heap of mess. But when it is finished, the building is made like the picture, but it is *bigger* and *nicer* than the actual picture they were showing. God says that is how we are. People may look at us while we are under construction. They may see a mess, but God is building us. He may have shown us who we are while we are under construction, but when we are finished being built, we will be bigger and nicer than what He showed us in our vision. The ministries that He has shown us that we are building are *bigger* and nicer than what we visualize.

Keeping the Focus on Him

Also, notice how people will keep watching as the building is going on? Same with us, people that see us under construction are watching. They are not saying anything, but they are watching out of curiosity. It is like they know something is coming soon. They can see us going through the fire. They can see us pressing and laboring hard. We do not have to climb on a rooftop with a megaphone and announce to the world that we are building something for God. Do any of the laborers that are on construction sites stand around taking selfies of themselves building and uploading the photos to social media? Do we see any construction workers going around bragging to others about what they are building? No, because when the work is done and the building is up and running, the focus is directed to the business, not the workers. It should be the same way with us when we are kingdom building.

Every time we brag/boast about what "we" are doing for the Lord, we are pulling the praise to ourselves. We want people to give us a "hand clap of praise," a pat on the back, recognize us for what we are doing for the Lord when all the attention should reflect to Him.

Again, He said to lift Him upon this earth, and He will draw all men unto Him, not us. It is not about us. Why do we feel we have to be recognized for what we do for the Lord? If we stop trying so hard to shine the spotlight on ourselves and praise the Lord for counting us worthy to even build for Him, maybe those who are in the darkness can believe God and receive salvation. *Selah!*

People are not converting to salvation as much anymore because of so many twisted things going on in the body of Christ. They may feel, why should they get saved when saved people are just as corrupt as the unsaved. We can let our light shine without taking the spotlight off God.

God showed me that little bit just from looking at the box of a jigsaw puzzle. Truth be told, when we take the puzzle out of the box, work on it and complete it; the puzzle is bigger than the picture on the box. God wants us to know that what we are doing for Him is *bigger* than what we imagine. He is a *big* God. He is a *mega* God. He is a *ginormous* God, and nothing He does is small. We have got to get it in our minds and our hearts just how *big* He *really* is. My God, that just blessed me. Speak Holy Spirit!

The actual thing is always better than the picture. It is the same as snapping a photo of a person. When we snap photos, we are only capturing snippets of who we really are. When we look at the photo, although we may have just taken it, the image is smaller than the actual "live" thing we captured. A photo cannot capture the *full detail* of us. Like the "coming soon" sites have nice photos, but when it is *completed*, it is bigger and more beautiful.

When we are completely matured in Christ, we will be more beautiful. It is bigger than what it is. So many times, people say we read too much into things. Sometimes we got to read more into things to get the actual substance from it. Some of us are not reaching our full potential because we are stuck in the *now* or the *what was* and do not realize we are a coming attraction. God has designed so much more for our lives. *Selah!*

Opening the Box

Opening the Box

Just as I was getting ready to assemble the jigsaw puzzle, I had to, of course, open the box and take the pieces out...

The Lord said, "Actions are loud sometimes, and you must pay attention to them because actions will tell you more about a person than words will."

Many months after I opened the puzzle box, the Lord brought back to me how I opened the box. Someone may be saying, "Gosh, it is just a box; how are you supposed to open it?". I thought the same thing. It never dawned on me that opening a simple box would effectively demonstrate an individual's actions towards things. The Lord spoke a simple word to me about opening the box that will forever stick with my spirit, and I hope and pray it does the same with the person reading this. I did not just open the box like I opened a box of cereal. I ripped the box open; I bit a hole in the plastic that the puzzle pieces were in. I tussled with it trying to gain the leverage I needed to open it up completely to pour out the pieces.

God showed me that when I open mail like my bills, a personal letter, or a check, it will take my time to open. I am careful about handling and opening that mail. However, when I open my junk mail, I handle it any kind of way. Frankly, I am not interested in what they are trying to sell me. When I open a box of cereal, I am careful to open it by the seal. When I open the bag that the cereal is in, I am careful not to rip it open. I take my time and open it (not bite a hole in it or cut it with scissors either). I handle the cereal bag gently because I want to make sure that it is sealed correctly to keep it fresh for the next usage.

God showed me how gentle we handle the things we care about, the things that we think are important to us. To me, at that time, the jigsaw puzzle assignment was not that important. When I first started the assignment, it was out of an act of obedience. My heart was not really into doing it. My actions showed where my heart was when I opened the box. It was far from doing that puzzle out of love. He also showed me through the box opening how aggressive I was with handling His sheep. I, impatiently and with an attitude of not wanting to be bothered, opened the box, and I did not care enough to accurately open the plastic it came in. I tore into it with my teeth. That is a huge error on my end that the Lord had to show me about myself.

God showed me that is how some of us are with the ministries He gives us. We may step up and take the assignment out of an act of obedience. For whatever reason, let the truth be told, our hearts may be far from the ministry God has ordered us to do. If we pay more attention, some of us can see it in our actions. A person's actions usually speak what is in their hearts.

Dear Pharisee and Sadducee Readers

The Lord is giving us *all* space to repent. Do not read this book with your noses in the air and miss the messages focusing on the messenger. "Repent! For the kingdom of heaven is at hand" (Matthew 4:17, KJV).

> *It is written*: "If we confess our sins, He is faithful and just to forgive us our sins and to cleanse us from all unrighteousness. If we say that we have not sinned, we make Him a liar, and His word is not in us" (1 John 1:9-10, KJV).

> "For all have sinned, and come short to the glory of God" (Romans 3:23, KJV).

Are we going to keep sitting up pointing the finger at the next person, or are we going to see what it is God is trying to show us about ourselves through the person who messed up so we can get ourselves together? And at the same time, pray for the person who messed up instead of throwing stones. Remember, the last section of this book spoke about trying to damage God's goods we cannot afford to fix or replace them. Do not try to condemn me. I am trying to help somebody here.

Anyway, God showed me that I was too aggressive, and I needed to tone it down. Now do not get it twisted; He allows me to be stern, bold for a reason. However, He was teaching me through a simple box how to be gentle and stern at the same time with ministry. When I had my children, I was stern with them. My children knew I did not play; however, I was also gentle with them, which assured them that I loved them. Kingdom-minded members need to know when to be authoritative and when to be gentle. We must know how to be both at the same time in leadership.

When we care more about the people, the ministry God has given us, we are more gentle and love more agape. We cannot just treat people like a puzzle box or a piece of junk mail. If we want to get the people to "open up" or in order to tap in to "open up" the people to what is going on inside, we must be gentle.

Some people are like onions, they have layers and layers of pain, and the more a person peels an onion, the closer the individual will get to the inside; the more it makes an individual cry. In ministry, some people may allow us to get close enough to them to peel the first layer off. If we rip it off like a band-aid on a wound, they are not going to trust us to go in a peel-off another layer. We must remember that in ministry, people are in pain. They are hurting, and they need someone to trust that they can share with. We cannot be running around here snatching open their boxes, amen.

We must pay attention to how we handle simple things daily, and God will show us things about ourselves that are dynamic. He will show us things about ourselves that may need some correction. If we want to be effective in ministry, we must make sure that we are effective ministers, amen. We have got to be careful how we "open the box."

Pouring Out What Is on the Inside

After opening the box, I poured the pieces on the table and saw all that I was working with, which was a lot. God showed me through the puzzle that we have so much more on the inside of us than what we can see on the outside. When people look at a puzzle box, they may just see the picture, but they may not comprehend what it took to put it together. They did not know what went on behind the scenes when we were putting the puzzle together. They did not know the time, laboring, pain, and frustration we went through to complete the puzzle. All they see is the finished product.

People of today do not take the time to get to know a person by their inside. All they want to know is how the outside look, and if it does not look appealing to them, then they may ridicule us and try to tear us down. If we would all take time to get to know one another, we would be surprised at what each of us got going on.

> *It is written*: "And we beseech you, brethren, to know them which labour among you, and are over you in the Lord, and admonish you" (1 Thessalonians 5:12, KJV).

We are all like the pieces to the jigsaw puzzle...

We are all puzzle pieces to His divine design. We are *the* Master's pieces.

Organizing the Pieces

Organizing the Pieces

That we henceforth be no more children, tossed to and fro, and carried about with every wind of doctrine, by the sleight of men, and cunning craftiness, whereby they lie in wait to deceive; but speaking the truth in love, may grow up into Him in all things, which is the head, even Christ: from whom the whole body fitly joined together and compacted by that which every joint supplieth, according to the effectual working in the measure of every part, maketh increase of the body unto the edifying of itself in love.

Ephesians 4:14-16 (KJV)

Before I could assemble the puzzle, I needed to organize the pieces. At the time of the assignment, organization was a part of the puzzle I did not have any notes on. However, the title was inducted into this book. It had an appointed time for me to write whatever the Lord wants me to speak at this precise moment about organization. From memory, I could not attempt to assemble the puzzle without first organizing the pieces.

I can hear the Lord say He gave us all our individual time. We are on His watch. His time and we are unorganized. He says that some of us are *wasting* His time. He gave us time to build this or do that, but we are *spending* the time He gave us on frivolous things. He says that many of us are *sleeping* away time. He says that some of us are *not strategizing* the time He gave us. He says that some of us, as the body of Christ, are unorganized. He says we have allowed division to hinder us from unifying and building. He says to imagine sitting down spending time assembling a jigsaw puzzle straight from the box. Imagine trying to find the pieces that we need without going through the process of turning over all the pieces or grouping the pieces. He says it would be harder for us to assemble the puzzle without first organizing it. He says that is how we are behaving now. He says there are too many of us trying to work alone when He has ordained teams to help us. He says many of us are not submitting to the leadership that He has ordained to watch over us. He says that many of us are trying to take charge when He did not authorize us to be in charge. He says many of us are not going to the streets, jailhouses, hospitals, shelters to compel His people to come home. He says the prodigals are still out wandering around. He wants His children that have backslidden to know that they can come home. He says that we are pushing more of self-ministry, glorifying ourselves more than we are Him. He said if He be lifted up, He will draw all men to Him. God says His body is out of order. He is the same yesterday, today, and forever. He says He did not place the woman over the man, but man head of the woman. He says some of the marriages in the body are not ordained by Him. He says He wants His body back the way He organized it from the beginning of time. He says to stop trying to change His design. Stop trying to change His plans. If we do not gather as one body and line up with His design, He will start to sift out the stiff necks by multitudes. We do not control Him; this is His divine design, and He will bring it back to His divine order with or without us. Let them that have ears to hear; hear what the Spirit of the Lord is saying right now and obey Him. Amen.

The Lord has given us life. He has given us a purpose for our lives. He has given us His time. He has given us everything we need to fulfill our divine purpose. He has given us an expected end. We need to reorganize our lives and line up with our divine purposes. He expects us to produce something from the time that He has given us. Our lives are not our own. Amen.

Flipping the Pieces

> "If you declare with your mouth, 'Jesus is Lord,' and believe in your heart that God raised Him from the dead, you will be saved. For it is with your heart that you believe and are justified, and it is with your mouth that you profess your faith and are saved" (Romans 10:9-10, NIV).

If you have not noticed by now, I am sure you can see that this book is pretty much detailed. Who would have thought that a simple jigsaw puzzle would have so much revelation to it concerning God's divine design that He has for our lives? Some people used to call me petty Betty and/or say I read too much into things, but I am so glad that the Lord reveals Himself to me through petty or simple things. Well, praise Jesus for a simple mind because it is the simple thing that God uses to confound the wise. Amen.

> *It is written*: "But God hath chosen the foolish things of the world to confound the wise; and God hath chosen the weak things of the world to confound the things which are mighty" (1 Corinthians 1:27, KJV).

After pouring the pieces on the table, I had to turn a lot of the pieces over. The Lord showed me through that portion of the demonstration that many times when we see the pieces that are *faced down*, it is hard to recognize where they belong. We cannot put the puzzle together with them faced down. This is the importance of letting our light shine when we are around the people of the world.

There were some pieces that were *already turned the right way*. God showed me, from turning over the pieces, there was ministry in that midst. He revealed to me that some of the people that are assigned to the same ministry as some of us are already saved, and most need to be turned over to Him!

He showed me that some of the pieces were *already connected*. He said that with some of the assignments that He gives us, some of the people will not be hard to find because we are already connected. He showed me in the puzzle that we have quite a few people attached to the ministry that He has already given to us. He is going to use us to turn them over, back to Him, back to the plan, back to the big picture. He said just because we cannot see their true colors in the beginning does not mean that they are not part of His plan.

He also showed me, in the different colors and shapes, that His body is not prejudiced. His divine design has a widespread of nationalities and denominations. Religious biases have crept into the body of Christ.

God showed me at the time of the puzzle assignment and still showing me how so many of His children are like the "flipping" puzzle pieces. The Lord showed me how we, the body of Christ, are around certain church people; we flip to the super saved saint. But as soon as we get in the church parking lot, we flip to the other side. We cannot get out of the church parking lot fast enough without cussing out our children, grabbing a cigarette, gossiping, or talking crazy to our spouses. We cannot keep flipping sides. God has created us to be a puzzle piece to connect to others, and they cannot connect to us because we are steady "flipping" sides. We are not just hindering our own walk; we are hindering those who are connected to us as well. It is time out for walking with God and holding hands with the devil. Either we are going to stay on one side, or we are going to stay on the other. God does not like lukewarm believers.

When we are flipping saints, that makes it hard for us to minister to other people, especially the unsaved; we cannot go and party, drink and get high with someone that is not saved, then turn around the next week with the church clan acting super saved trying to save the ones we just partied with the week before. We cannot cuss and fuss with our spouses then turn around and try to speak an edifying word to them. They are going to reject it. We have got to stop going out in the name of the Lord and shaming His name. We have got to stop being those "flipping pieces" and start focusing on helping flip over the pieces that need to be flipped over. We must stop acting like unsaved Christians, so we can help save the unbelievers in Jesus' name. We need to stop dimming our light. Stop flipping to the other side. Stop trying to blend in with the cardboard side and operate in our true colors. Doing so, the cardboard side will want to flip over to the other side as well. Amen.

Also, we must be mindful of the cardboard side pieces. Many believers mistreat people because they do not know that the cardboard-sided person has beautiful colors on the other side and belongs to God's divine design as well. It is not up to us to decide who can be in His divine design. There may be a homeless alcoholic living under a bridge that needs to be "flipped" to the other side. But because they look or smell bad, a believer may feel like they should not be offered salvation. Jesus did say go to the hedges and the highways and compel them to come in.

> *It is written*: "Then the master told his servant, 'Go out to the roads and country lanes and compel them to come in, so that my house will be full'" (Luke 14:23, NIV).

We, as the body of Christ, need to stop looking at the cardboard side of people and see the colorful divine design side of them. That alcoholic, drug user, drug dealer, gambler, prostitute, murderer, homosexual may be pieces to His perfect design. God did say He will have mercy and compassion on whom He wants to.

> *It is written*: "For He says to Moses, 'I will have mercy on whom I have mercy, and I will have compassion on whom I have compassion'" (Romans 9:15, NIV).

We should not be so quick to judge who should be "flipped" over. Amen.

Familiarizing

God showed me that in ministry, it is important to familiarize ourselves with the people that we are going to build with. It is vital.

We cannot be out on the battlefield with loaded guns as our weapons, and we expect the ones that are building with us to have loaded guns as well, but they come out to battle with butter knives. We must be on one accord with our builders. Sometimes we may say, "I do not connect with him or her," and it may be that the reason why we are not connecting is because they may be connected to the wrong people. If God placed us on an assignment together, they are our connection. It may be wise to check the people they are connected to that is making our connection bad with them. It is vital to know our surroundings.

Hidden Pieces

After flipping all the pieces over to the right side, I began separating them and familiarizing myself with the different colors and shapes. I began to place all the corner pieces in a group together, and all the colors that looked alike, I placed them in their groups.

He also showed me that after separating the different puzzle pieces and putting them in different piles, I still had to go in the piles to look for certain pieces because they were not in the piles that they belonged in. Sometimes the Lord will allow us to be hidden during an assignment. He allows us to be hidden until our appointed time to come forth. Some of us try so hard to be seen so we can be used, but we must realize that it is not time yet. God has a special time for us to be revealed and used for His glory. He said that many times we get overlooked with our heavenly assignment, but do not fret because, regardless, we will be used. What He has for us is for us. We can be pushed to the side, placed in other groups, put in a box, etc. but at the end of the day, when it is all said and done, they will be looking for us to complete the assignment, and we should not be arrogant about them needing us because we need them as well.

There is an appointed time before we are revealed and released in ministry. We cannot rush God to use us. Just as the puzzle pieces that were hidden in the middle of the other pieces and had to wait until their appointed time to be used, so do we, as members in the body of Christ. The hidden pieces were in the middle of the design. They were a part of the plan. They had a purpose for the plan. The design could not be completed without the puzzle pieces fulfilling their divine purpose. No other pieces could fit where they belonged. They were designed to fit in a specific spot of the design. Same with us as the body of Christ. The Lord may be hiding us for a season. We already have a purpose for His divine design. We are originals. No one can fit where God has already designed us to be. Remember, we always say, "What God has for me is for me." We are merely confessing that we have been tailor-made for His plan. We must wait until our appointed time for Him to use us however He wants to. This is His plan, His design. Amen.

Blending Pieces

Sometimes we might meet some unbelievers and feel a strong connection. The spirit of God in us is telling us that they are our lost siblings that need to be offered salvation. Some of the pieces that have not been turned (saved) yet are connected to His divine design. There is a reason why we feel the connection to some of them. However, we cannot try to blend in with them because if we do, we are turning our puzzle pieces to the other side. The blind cannot lead the blind.

How does it look to be this beautifully colorful puzzle piece and the Lord sends us to the streets to get some of the other puzzle pieces that are faced down, or He may send us into a family gathering to show our beautiful colors, and we sit up and blend in with the crowd. Cussing, drinking, talking ungodly language, and gossiping. How is that helping them? By blending in the midst of darkness for the wrong purpose, we are allowing our light to be either dimmed or put out.

Sometimes we may go too far by compromising, and the next thing is they have flipped us to the cardboard side of the puzzle, the colorless side, a faced-down puzzle piece. We have got to let our light shine in the middle of darkness, or the darkness may overshadow our light. We cannot play with *the* light. Amen.

Unwanted Pieces/Workers

Imagine this: There is a puzzle on a table unfinished because the person who is working on it thinks that some of the parts to the puzzle do not belong. They tossed the unwanted parts of the puzzle to the side. But little did they know that the puzzle could not be completed without those voided parts.

Same with the body of Christ. Some of us have in our minds that some members are not worthy of being a part because of whatever sin/wrong that member may have done. Or maybe we just do not like the member and do not want to do ministry with them. We may attempt to avoid that person by shutting them out of our lives. Then, we wonder why it is hard to complete the ministries that were given to us. It is not for us to decide who should and should not be a part of kingdom building. Sometimes we will pray and ask God to send someone to help us build when He had already sent help when He gave us the assignment. Because we did not like who He sent, we took it upon ourselves and tossed them away, closed them out, wrote them off.

The Lord is saying to the individuals that are reading this right now, you know who you are. The Lord says for you to go back and get that missing puzzle piece, that much-needed member that you thought you did not need to help us to build. You are wrong, and you need to be told that you have put too many puzzle pieces away thinking about your own selfish desires. Talking about "my ministry." No, it is not "your" ministry. It is God's ministry, and He may have placed you as steward over it. You let it go to your head and threw away too many pieces attached to that puzzle, baby. God did not tell you to do that. You were in your feelings, and now your feelings cannot get the puzzle (building assignment) completed because you threw out or lost some puzzle pieces you need to complete the puzzle. Humble yourself and go apologize and bring those people back to complete His assignment. Amen.

The Lord says to us, the body of Christ, to stop getting in our feelings on the job and build. Stop leaning to our own understanding. Stop trying to override His authority. Stop trying to design our own plan. It is not going to work. The Lord says to stop mishandling His people. The main ones we think are the least in the body are the most effective members. The ones we think are the least, God will show more favor towards just because. Remember how Jacob mistreated Leah and God favored her over Rachel with baring children. Jacob did not treat Leah as he treated Rachel, and because so, God showed Leah more favor by giving her six sons and a daughter. We must be careful how we handle one another.

Stealing Pieces

God showed me how He sends people to us to say something uplifting, prophetic to us, and it is like they came in our life to put pieces of the puzzle together inside of us that we could not find. He also showed me how some people come in and see us working on our "self" puzzle, and they try to steal a piece or pieces to our puzzle so we cannot complete what is being built on the inside of us. Sometimes we allow people to come in and steal our hope, erupt our visions, and trample over our peace. That is the enemy coming in, taking away pieces to our "self" puzzle that we may have already found and put together. I see the enemy has come in and stolen the "joy" and "self-esteem" puzzle pieces from a lot of God's people. I see him snatching the "dignity" pieces and replacing them with imitation pieces.

Trading Pieces/Prayer

He is giving "pride" and "bitterness" pieces in place of the pieces he has stolen. He is connecting "perversion" and "lasciviousness" to the pieces to the "self" puzzle, but I bind him now in the name of Jesus. We have got to stop trading puzzle pieces with the devil. He has been exposed, and I say, Satan, lose my brother and my sister's puzzle pieces now in the name of Jesus and give them back their rightful pieces in the name of Jesus. You cannot take what does not belong to you, but you better take back what does. Take back your bitterness, perversion, homosexuality, lasciviousness. Take back your pride. We are children of the highest God, and pride does not rest in us; unforgiveness, identity confusion, and bitterness are not a part of the puzzle. Take it back in the name of Jesus. Give back these people dignity in the name of Jesus, amen.

God gave us everything we need on the inside of us, and we need to take the time to build/put the pieces together. We must stop trying to take shortcuts and get to work. We must be careful not to allow the enemy to use us to snatch pieces away from our siblings in Christ. We must *build* one another up. You may be a spiritual puzzle piece I need one day to come and speak something edifying to me. Do not come and pull one of my pieces out and mess up my puzzle. Come help me build it, amen.

The Differences Between Cut Off and Disconnected Pieces

The Differences Between Cut Off and Disconnected Pieces

There was a time the Lord had me create some big puzzle pieces from a cardboard box and demonstrate His Word by showing His people what it looks like when we cut off connections with people God gave to us for kingdom-building purposes. It was demonstrated by showing how most puzzle pieces have four to six connections to one piece, and if we connect one of the pieces to the wrong piece, it will offset the whole connection. Other people cannot connect to us because we may have somewhere connected to a wrong person.

God showed me how some women love to hold grudges. We may be connected to someone who may be a wrong connection. We may have a disagreement and may stop speaking to one another. Instead of disconnecting ourselves from the wrong connection/person, we will break off the whole connection so no one else can connect to us to prevent us from getting hurt again. We will shut down and shut everyone else out. We are being selfish by cutting off the whole connection. It is wrong and ungodly. It is an act of bitterness.

Wrong Connections

Sometimes it happens, when we connect ourselves to the wrong people, we have got to learn how to disconnect ourselves and still be open to connecting with the right people. When we break off that little head to the puzzle that is enabling us to connect to someone else, we are preventing them from connecting to the ones they need to connect to.

This is not about us, and we need not be selfish and bitter about it when someone disappoints and hurt us. Sometimes God allows them to hurt us anyway because He has told us over and over either not to connect with them or to let them go because they cannot go where we are going. But we lean to our own understanding and stay connected. When God allows them to sting us, we crawl up in our little shells and do not want to trust anyone else. We have got to trust God and stop linking up with *wrong* connections.

God showed me through the puzzle that we can be in the church and have a lot in common, but still may not be the right connections. Just because we go to the same church and serving the same God does not mean that we should be "directly" connected. I may be a piece of the sky, and you may be a piece of the barn. I cannot make you connect directly to me.

Prejudice Believers

Some of us in some churches are like that. God has churches all around the planet, and some of us think because we go to the same church or the church's we are affiliated with are the only connections to the puzzle. God may be using someone in China to connect with us to build. We have got to familiarize ourselves with the pieces to the puzzle and stop being "prejudice" saints. We must stop being closed-minded about fellowshipping with other believers in this world.

> *It is written*: "From one man He made all the nations, that they should inhabit the whole earth; and He marked out their appointed times in history and the boundaries of their lands" (Acts 17:26, NIV).

We preach to the sinners that God is love and to stop being prejudice, but the church is the main one that is prejudice. United we stand, divided we fall. Lucifer and his army sure are not divided. They all stand together to tear down the children of God. Let the truth be told; they really do not have much work to do because we sit up day in and year out fighting each other and dividing the churches into denominations and nationalities. That is not of God. Oh, I feel the stones; be careful, stone-throwers, remember we cannot afford to fix anything we damage or break that belongs to God.

Certain people in the churches get in their special little groups and will not let anyone in. God showed me that sometimes when we group the pieces and start working on the puzzle, oftentimes, the wrong pieces are in the wrong groups. Just because we click well with someone does not mean that we are on a *direct* building assignment. We have got to stop expecting to build with the same people every time. God may have a different position for each of us on the next assignment. Some of the members will not allow other members to be partakers of their ministry because it is only for certain members. That is not God. That is sign of an occult.

God says we have got to stop thinking mediocre and take Him out of the box. He is trying to show us bigger, but we are so caught up in the familiar. When He is saying we are familiar with the bigger too, but we are too scared to "come up hither." Scared that we are going to fail at something we have never tried before, so we want to stick with what we are good at. Not knowing that He made us better at what we are scared to step up to.

We must know that there are always higher heights and deeper depths when we are dealing with God.

We should not get caught up in groups that we do not belong in. Nor should we mix ourselves with people that are not growing or going where we are growing and going. We may have been with them last season, but this season God is calling us higher in Him. We should be thinking big because we serve a big God. For the readers that already are, the Lord says to think bigger in Jesus' name, amen.

Protecting the Pieces
Brother/Sister Keepers

One thing about assembling a puzzle, if we lose a piece, it will throw off the whole puzzle, making it incomplete. When I think about this, I think about the parable Jesus told about the hundred sheep and the one that strayed away, and He said if that one is lost, you leave the ninety-nine in the wilderness and go after the one lost until you find it.

> *It is written*: "Suppose one of you has a hundred sheep and loses one of them. Doesn't he leave the ninety-nine in the open country and

go after the lost sheep until he finds it?" (Luke 15:4, NIV).

It reminds me of the parable of the woman who lost her coin.

It is written: "Suppose a woman has ten silver coins[a] and loses one. Doesn't she light a lamp, sweep the house and search carefully until she finds it?" (Luke 15:8, NIV).

When assembling a puzzle, if one piece is lost, we are going to look all around until we find that one missing piece. It may bother us that we have sat up and spent all our time fixing a puzzle only to find out that a piece is missing. We know the piece is somewhere near because when we bought the puzzle, all the pieces were included. A puzzle is not more important than us. If we care enough to look for a lost puzzle piece or we care enough to be careful not to lose any pieces to the puzzle, we should care the same about each other. It is our duty as kingdom siblings to look out for one another. We are our brothers and sisters' keepers. We must handle one another with care, protecting each other, and look out for one another. If one of us may lose our way, we are supposed to go out and look for the lost one until we find them and bring them back. Jesus said to leave the ninety-nine and go look for the one lost. How many of us notice that a member has been missing from service and decide to reach out and call or go visit them? Many of us today will not go after that lost sheep, not even when the Lord tells us to go after them. Nine times out of ten, some of us are glad the member left anyway. It is a sad thing to say, but it is the truth that needs to be told to shame the devil. Body of Christ, we must do right by the lost sheep and go out to check on them, encourage them, compel them to come back home to the Lord. We must show agape love.

Assembling Time

Assembling Time

"I have posted watchmen on your walls, Jerusalem; they will never be silent day or night. You who call on the Lord, give yourselves no rest, and give him no rest till he establishes Jerusalem and makes her the praise of the earth"

(Isaiah 62:6-7, NIV).

Outside First

When assembling a puzzle, most of us will start with the outside pieces first. The outside pieces are easier to put together; once assembled, it is easier to connect the other pieces. The assorted colors also make it easier to connect the pieces.

The outside pieces do not have as many connections as the pieces on the inside. When I was studying the outside pieces, I heard the Lord say the reason why the outside pieces do not have outer connections is to protect the inside pieces from connecting to the wrong pieces to other puzzles. God told me that the outside pieces represent leadership, and it is easier putting those pieces together. He said, when we are leaders, we are strong and should know better. No one should have to hold our hand or tell us to do this or that. No one should have to tell us who the bad connections are. When we are in leadership, it is our job to protect the inside connections (the sheep) and to keep the ministry together.

Think of it, if we have a puzzle where there are all kinds of connections sticking out and no borders, we are leaving the puzzle open for other puzzle pieces to attempt to come in and connect to the puzzle when they already know that they are not a part of the puzzle. It is important to seal in the open connections because sometimes pieces may fit the connection, but they do not fit the picture (plan). Amen.

Sometimes members get upset when the members in leadership do not get in the "center" of things that are taking place in the church. The members want the leaders to come out and join in with the rest of the congregation on the inside, but if leaders were always in the midst of the members on the inside, who will be on watch to protect us from the wolves on the outside?

There are some that may say there are wolves on the inside, and the watchmen need to protect them from the wolves. We must realize that just as there are wolves in sheep clothing, there may sometimes be sheep in wolves clothing. We all have something we have battled with or still battling. It is the job of the members on the inside to help the others on the inside that may portray to be a wolf. Remember, the Lord does not look at the outward appearance. He looks at the heart. He also said to walk by faith and not by sight. Looks are deceiving.

Sometimes we buy puzzles from off the shelf brand new and open them up and find out that there are defective pieces in the midst, but that does not mean that they do not belong. It is our job to build together, to accept one another as God has accepted us. If we are inside pieces to the puzzle, we need to stop acting like the corner pieces. We need to stop ridiculing the corner pieces as well. Throwing stones at our leaders because God set them apart to watch over the ministry, and it is not a cup of tea.

When God shows those that He authorized to be watchmen over our souls something, and they try to tell us, we should not cast them off as the "holier than thou" or "know it all" saints. They are the seers, watchmen, shepherds of our souls. We, as members in the body of Christ, must stop getting upset when our leaders/watchmen are not able to partake in some church festivities. We need to not be offended and understand them when they exclude themselves.

It is vital that the edge pieces connect with all the other edge pieces and know that just because we are all edge pieces does not mean that we all see the same thing. We are still different. Remember there are edge pieces that are the sky, trees, water, flowers, etc. We should not doubt other edge pieces or fight with them, trying to be the bigger edge piece. We are all needed for His divine design. It is truly time to walk in unity. Note to the outside pieces. Know that you are not the only ones on the outside. There are people that you can connect to that are like you. They are watchmen and seers too. Do not get upset when the Lord does not allow you to attend certain church events (dinners, birthday parties, after church feasts, etc.) that the inside pieces are going to. Do not get upset when you are unable to connect/allow a lot of people in your space as the inside members/connections do. Do not grow weary in well-doing. God designed you to be a watchman on the wall, a seer, a protector/shepherd. He made you to be strong to hold up the inside pieces. Also, know that someone is always praying for you, even when you do not know it. Amen.

The edge pieces are made like a wall for a reason. The enemy will attempt to come with force to knock down the wall to get in where the other puzzle pieces (sheep) are, but God has given the shepherds/watchmen/outer puzzle pieces a supernatural strength made of steel to take a licking and keep on ticking. The more the enemy bang on, beat on, throw stones, bombs, darts everything, including the kitchen sink at the wall, the watchmen are still there standing tall, protecting the other pieces (the sheep). Not one booby trap sent from the enemy will prevail.

The inside pieces do not have a clue of the battles that the outside pieces have going on. The inside pieces do not have a clue of the warfare; the demons the outside pieces battle with to protect the inside pieces. They tend to ridicule leadership, talk down on us, tell us that we think we are better than them, but we are not. They may step on us, throw us under the bus, call us every name in the book, but a child of God. They truly do not have a clue of how much love the outside pieces have for them, and sometimes we, as the leadership, must be stern with the sheep because we see some things that the sheep cannot see. It is our job to protect the sheep.

They do not understand, and we/the leaders should not get bitter about it or take any of it to heart but thank God for counting us worthy to be an edge piece to the puzzle. We are stronger than we think we are.

My prayer for those in leadership, the watchmen, the outer puzzle pieces, I pray that God gives us a fresh anointing and that we continue to stand because we are much needed in this divine design. If we are moved, if we give up, if we step down, we are leaving an opening for the enemy to slither his way in to harm/contaminate/poison the other puzzle pieces. May the Lord give us a double portion of a supernatural strength to endure it all without fainting or complaining. May we continue to labor in agape love all for the glory of God in Jesus' name, amen.

All who are in leadership, it is time to get along, and *kingdom build* all to the glory of God. All our gifts *will* make room for us, amen. Let us *all* walk in *unity* in Jesus' name.

Following Instructions

We need to stop leaning to our own understanding and take the limits off God when it comes to our gifts. Also, when we force connections, it makes it harder for everyone else to complete their assignment. Let me say this while it is fresh on my mind. Assignment, how many times have we, as children of God, used that word? When God gives us an assignment, He gives us the instructions as well. When we went to school, our teachers gave us an assignment and the instructions for the assignment as to how they wanted or expected it to be done. What makes us think we can work on something without the instructions? *Selah!*

That is another thing that is wrong with the body of Christ now. Nobody wants to follow instructions, but we are steady saying we have "assignments" from God. What kind of foolishness is it to do something without reading the instructions or listening to the person who does have the instructions for the assignment? We need to cut that mess out. I tell you the truth; we will not go to a construction site and see construction workers just building without the instructions from the one holding the blueprint. *Selah!*

God will give one of our siblings in Christ an assignment, and we may be called in to help complete the assignment, but nobody wants to hear the plans from the visionary. The person God placed in charge. Why? Because somewhere deep down, there is pride. The ole Leviathan and Jezebel spirits are lying dormant. As soon as one of our siblings in Christ attempts to do something positive for the Lord, that Jezebel/controlling spirit will try to slip in and take over everything, trying to control everybody, especially if an individual is operating in the Jezebel spirit that has been there for a while. The spirit will think that it has more right to control the assignment than the member God has chosen to do. That Jezebel spirit will control that individual's mind having our sibling in Christ thinking that he or she has the right to control it all, but God is a God that sits up high and looks low, and He sees and knows all. Many say, "God knows my heart." He sure does, and that is why many of us were not chosen to hold the instructions for the assignment because of our stinking thinking. God shall get *all* the glory. He is not sharing it with anyone.

Another thing that is fresh on my mind is the following: it is truly time out for all this division, self-righteous, big "I," and little "u" foolishness. We are all a part of God's body, and it is time for us to come together in unity and be about it. We all need each other in one way or another to *kingdom build*. We need to stop bickering, arguing, and fighting and start to get along. It is time out for shaming God's name. Enough already! In Jesus' name, amen.

Laying the Foundation

When you are assembling a jigsaw puzzle, some may take longer than the next to put together. Me, personally, when I was putting the puzzle together, I spent a lot of time working on it. I would work on it until I got frustrated or tired, then I would stop, but I was determined to complete the puzzle. There were some days I would see the puzzle on the table, and I was like, "I do not feel like finishing it." However, I refused to start once again something without finishing it. I decided to strategize my time. I said I would work on it before or after such and such, and I was going to work on it for two maybe three hours, or I was going to keep working on certain areas until all the pieces were together. When I decided to do it that way, I noticed that I was less frustrated, and I was seeing the fruit of my labor being manifested.

Also, that was during the time I began to think about all the hard work I had been putting into the puzzle. It was on my coffee table. I began to think and said I was not going to put the puzzle together, and it ended up falling apart, I did not want to lose pieces, or I had to move it for whatever reason. So, I came up with the conclusion to get a solid board and some glue and glue all the pieces together so it could be permanent.

God showed me that should have been one of the first things I did before I started putting the puzzle together. He showed me that some of us have been building ministries that do not have *solid foundations*. Before putting the puzzle together, before pouring out the pieces, we must make sure there is a solid foundation to build on. We cannot put a puzzle together on a bed or something soft. We must put it together on something solid.

In the body of Christ, we must always build on solid foundations, or whatever we build will crumble and fall. Jesus, the Word is our solid foundation. We must build on the Word. Amen.

Imagine this: You have been working on your jigsaw puzzle at the kitchen table for hours, days, weeks, months, and the time has come that you need the space and the puzzle must be moved...you cannot move it without it falling apart. All the time you have spent laboring and putting the puzzle together has now been wasted because you did not have it on a solid foundation. You did have it on a foundation, but it was not solid!

God says that is what we are doing with His ministries. There are some places that He has told us to build (solid foundations), but we may not want to build in those places due to leaning to our own understanding. God may say, "Build at this church" or "that house" or "over there," but because we do not like certain things that are going on in the church; or we do not like certain locations, because they may be less than what we are used to; we might not want to go to that sister or brother house; or we may not want to build here or there because of this or that, and choose to build where we think it suitable to build and expect God to honor it, and God is saying, "I will make it like quicksand. The next time I tell you to build somewhere specific, and you disobey Me and attempt to build somewhere else, I will *not supply* the lumber or the laborers to help you build. I will not supply the equipment. You will not waste anything else of Mine because you do not want to obey Me." Saith the Lord.

Imagine this: You are an engineer/architect, and you have supplied all the equipment to build the design that is blue-printed out, and you have chosen the location to build and hired your workers. You go to the location where you told them to build, and they are not there. When you finally find your workers, they are at another location building with your equipment with different workers and a different design. They have made their own blueprint and building what they want to build and where they want to build with your stuff. Now that just made me cry. God is not a wimp. We are not going to be taking His gifts He has given us and operating in them wherever we want to and how we want to. Yes, the gifts come without repentance, and it is good to operate in them, but God is trying to get us to build something far greater than the mediocre mess we are sitting up building...with His stuff...how dare we do Him like that?

Oowee, forgive us, Lord, thank You for Your love and Your enduring mercy. You have constantly endured our *mess*. Forgive us, Abba Father. Lord, help us to obey You and build in the specific locations You have assigned to us in Jesus' name. Lord, please do not let us build on quicksand. Lord, we do not want to build in puddles of mud either. Lord, help us to heed Your Word and not lean to our own understanding and go where You say go and build in Jesus' name, amen.

The Lord has given some of us kingdom finances to build with, and we spent the money on other things that were not even kingdom.

Let me tell the truth and shame the devil. I am one who used to love nice things. I loved my home looking nice and cozy. I had just purchased a brand-new living room set for my birthday back in 2016 after waiting almost a year and finally coming into the money to pay cash for one. I had also just brought a car, was not brand new, but it was a good running car, and it was mine, no payments. The Lord spoke to me six months after I had purchased new items for my home, and I was planning to redecorate. He said, "Sale everything." Immediately I thought He was about to uproot me and send me to another location. I did as He said, and I sold everything in my home. I really thought that the Lord was about to move me out of town, but the purpose for me having to get rid of everything was to focus on the ministries He had ahead for me and to write three books He had been telling me to write for years. He did not tell me to take that money I had come into and spend it on furniture and a car. I did not ask Him first. I just spent. And He just said, "Get rid of it all." I had lost my focus. I had too many distractions around me. I now see that I had taken His kingdom's finances and purchased what I wanted for my apartment. He had given me the money to produce a ministry in a certain place. At the time, I did not know the money was for ministry purposes. All I was thinking about was I was standing in need of new furniture and a vehicle because I was tired of riding the city bus. I messed up, and the Lord made me get rid of everything I had purchased. The sad thing is, I did not have the items long, and when I sold them, I did not get half the amount I paid for. The sadder thing is the gathering He told me to produce did not happen because I spent the seed money on myself.

Wait a minute, let me clear the air. The seed money was income tax money, and school refund came at the same time. I figured because it was my school money and tax money, I could buy what I thought I needed. Nope! God had other plans, and I failed to seek Him about them before I spent the money. Big mistake. Big lesson learned. I allowed that lump sum of money to blind-side me. God fixed that real quick. Made me get rid of it all. I could not see then, but I sure can see now. Thank the Lord for His tender mercies.

It is truly time out for being stubborn and not wanting to go here or there and not wanting to work with him or her. When it is all said and done, we are going to have to connect to complete His divine design.

The Fruits of the Spirit

The Fruits of the Spirit

"But the fruit of the Spirit is love, joy, peace, longsuffering, gentleness, goodness, faith, meekness, temperance: against such there is no law"

(Galatians 5:22-23, KJV).

God had given me a five-hundred-piece puzzle to complete for one of many reasons; He was dealing with me personally about my patience. It appeared to me as if it were going to take forever for me to complete the puzzle. I had grown restless. I would get annoyed when I could not find the right pieces to fit the design. I complained about it taking too long. My joy was interrupted, and so was my peace. I was throwing the puzzle pieces back in the box or on the table. I was banging them with my fist. I wanted to quit.

The Lord was teaching me naturally and spiritually how I was far from walking in the nine fruit of the spirit. He said if we are going to be employed for Him, we must have the nine fruit of the spirit *skills*. In ministry, there is a lot of laboring. He said the harvest is plentiful, and the laborers are few. There is plenty of work to do and not enough laborers.

> *It is written*: "He told them, 'The harvest is plentiful, but the workers are few. Ask the Lord of the harvest, therefore, to send out workers into His harvest field'" (Luke 10:2, NIV).

He said that some of us will have to labor longer than others. He does not have the time for His skilled laborers to be murmuring and complaining or falling short with the kingdom movement. He said it is imperative to operate in the nine fruit of the spirit, which are love, joy, peace, longsuffering, gentleness, goodness, faithfulness, meekness, and temperance (Galatians 5:22-23).

Love

"There is no fear in love; but perfect love casteth out fear: because fear hath torment. He that feareth is not made perfect in love" (1 John 4:18, KJV).

No matter how much I thought I was showing love, it was not good enough. Everyone I said, "I love you," rejected me. When I showed love to people, I was misunderstood, and people shut me out. I did not understand what I was doing wrong. What was wrong with the love I had to offer? Why were people rejecting it? I was pretty much bowing down to the individuals I loved. I was trying everything to satisfy them, even if it made me miserable in the process. I felt like I was walking on eggshells around them. It seemed that I could not do or say anything right to please them. I was always rejected. Sometimes, I would love others so hard that I would find myself in situations I knew I would not have been in if I would not have tried everything to satisfy those people. I was miserable. I felt like I was being tormented by the people I really loved. So, I backed up. I shut down. I had realized that I was trying to love God's people through my own might.

The Lord had to rebuild me in that area because, no matter how much I had been rejected, I could never stop loving people. My heart just will not allow it, however, because I was wounded in this area. I had trust issues and did not want the love I had in my heart for others to manifest. At times, I was scared to tell and show others that I loved them. I feared that if they knew I loved them, they would use it against me. I feared that they would use my love to manipulate me to give them things for me to be able to stay in their lives. I feared that if I told them that I loved them, I would not get the same answer in return. I feared that if I showed love, I would be thought of as a weakling. I was not operating in God's *perfect* love. Perfect love cast out *all* fear (1 John 4:18).

When we love through our own strength, we may condition our love towards the individual. If they do something we do not like or if they hurt our feelings, we may place a halt on the love or renege the love we claimed we had for the individual.

God wants us to show *agape* love, His love to others. Agape love does not have conditions. God's love is unconditional. God's love looks past the faults. God wants us to love without fear. The Lord wants us to love one another as Christ loves the church. God said if we love Him, we must love our siblings in Him too. He has commanded us to love one another.

> *It is written*: "Love is patient, love is kind. It does not envy, it does not boast, it is not proud. It does not dishonor others, it is not self-seeking, it is not easily angered, it keeps no record of wrongs. Love does not delight in evil but rejoices with the truth. It always protects, always trusts, always hopes, always perseveres. Love never fails" (1 Corinthians 13:4-8, NIV).

> *It is written*: "Follow God's example, therefore, as dearly loved children and walk in the way of love, just as Christ loved us and gave Himself up for us as a fragrant offering and sacrifice to God" (Ephesians 5:1-2, NIV).

> *It is written*: "Dear friends, let us love one another, for love comes from God. Everyone who loves has been born of God and knows God. Whoever does not love does not know God, because God is love. This is how God showed His love among us: He sent His one and only Son into the world that we might live through Him. This is love: not that we loved God, but that He loved us and sent His Son as an atoning sacrifice for our sins. Dear friends, since God so loved us, we also ought to love one another. No one has ever seen God; but if we love one another, God lives in us and His love is made complete in us" (1 John 4:7-12 NIV).

> *It is written*: "We love because He first loved us. Whoever claims to love God yet hates a brother or sister is a liar. For whoever does not love their brother and sister, whom they have seen, cannot love God, whom they have not seen. And He has given us this command: Anyone who loves God must also love their brother and sister" (1 John 4:19-2, NIV).

Joy

> "[t]he joy of the Lord is your strength" (Nehemiah 8:10, KJV).

There is nothing more the devil wants to do than to kill, steal and destroy our joy. If we are happy, trusting in the Lord, the devil is mad. We can wake up one morning happy. As we go throughout the day, things may begin to happen to us that may disturb, interfere with our joy. The devil wants us miserable, doubting God, in bondage. If we lack joy, we may fall weak to the enemy's plot against us.

The Lord already knows what the outcome will be for each day of our lives. He planned it out already. There is absolutely nothing that can catch God by surprise. He tells us over and over to trust Him and to rejoice; He got this! We have no reason to feel sad when things happen to us. We should lift our hands and say, "Thank You, Lord, I am still going to be joyful. I am still going to worship You because I know that this, too, is a part of Your divine plan for my life. Amen." We must trust Him with everything in us. We must stop allowing the enemy to steal our joy. There is plenty of word from God to assure us that *He got this*!

It is written: "My brethren, count it all joy when ye fall into divers temptations; knowing this, that the trying of your faith worketh patience" (James 1:2-3, KJV).

It is written: "Wherein ye greatly rejoice, though now for a season, if need be, ye are in heaviness through manifold temptations: that the trial of your faith, being much more precious than of gold that perisheth, though it be tried with fire, might be found unto praise and honour and glory at the appearing of Jesus Christ: whom having not seen, ye love; in whom, though now ye see Him not, yet believing, ye rejoice with joy unspeakable and full of glory: receiving the end of your faith, even the salvation of your souls" (1 Peter 1:6-9, KJV).

It is written: "For His anger endureth but a moment; in His favour is life: weeping may endure for a night, but joy cometh in the morning" (Psalm 30:5, KJV).

It is written: "This is the day which the Lord hath made; we will rejoice and be glad in it" (Psalm 118:24, KJV).

It is written: "Rejoice in the Lord always: and again, I say, Rejoice" (Philippians 4:4, KJV).

It is written: "For the kingdom of God is not meat and drink; but righteousness, and peace, and joy in the Holy Ghost" (Romans 14:17, KJV).

It is written: "Trust in the Lord with all thine heart; and lean not unto thine own understanding. In all thy ways acknowledge Him, and He shall direct thy paths" (Proverbs 3:5-6, KJV).

Again, the Lord says rejoice, every day, trust Him. He got this!

Peace

"Peace I leave with you, My peace I give unto you: not as the world giveth, give I unto you. Let not your heart be troubled, neither let it be afraid"

(John 14:27, KJV).

While working on the puzzle assignment, the Lord showed me how I allowed ministry, itself, to frustrate me and how I would lose my joy and peace in the process. He showed me how I was beating up the people, trying to make them understand the importance of His Word and living Holy. I would get offended when they would not receive what I was sharing with them. I felt like I was failing Him. How many of us also know that we cannot make people obey God? We need to make sure our hands are clean and that we obey Him.

The weights of the world always come to interrupt our peace. The biggest peace breaker, I believe, outside of ministry right now, is the telemarketing calls. I believe Satan himself uses spam callers to dial our numbers all day long just to knock us out of our peace zones. Not only does he send the attacks through the audio dialer, he now sends them through text messages and emails, trying to overwhelm our eye and ear gates and trying to break our joy and peace.

If we always keep our minds on Him, nothing can take our peace away. We must let the peace of God rule our hearts. We must wear our shoes of peace everywhere we go (Ephesians 6:15). Below are a few scriptures to meditate on when we feel our peace is being interrupted. There are several scriptures concerning peace. Please feel free to research. However, these are the scriptures I was led to insert in this book at *this appointed time.*

> *It is written*: "Thou wilt keep him in perfect peace, whose mind is stayed on Thee: because he trusteth in Thee" (Isaiah 26:3, KJV).

> *It is written*: "And let the peace of God rule in your hearts, to the which also ye are called in one body; and be ye thankful" (Colossians 3:15, KJV).

> *It is written*: "Great peace have they which love Thy law: and nothing shall offend them" (Psalm 119:165, KJV).

> *It is written*: "For to be carnally minded is death; but to be spiritually minded is life and peace" (Romans 8:6, KJV).

> *It is written*: "Blessed are the peacemakers: for they shall be called the children of God" (Matthew 5:9, KJV).

Longsuffering

Another pitfall I learned about myself was, I hated to suffer for a long time. If something took too long for me and I was steadily suffering, I ended up complaining. God showed me the error of my ways. I was just like Moses and the Israelites. I always ended up in the wilderness longer than I should have been. It was all the murmuring and complaining I was doing that kept me in my trials extra long.

If we are in the middle of a trial, the worst thing we could do is complain while we are in the trial. It will only prolong the process. God wants us to be free from complaining. However long God chooses to allow us to go through something, we still should be grateful for Him counting us worthy to be tried. Job was a good man in good standings with God (Job 2:3). He was minding his own business, but God allowed him to be tried by the devil. Job suffered long and hard. His own wife told him, "Man, just curse God and die already." Job had to be unprepossessing for his own wife to tell him that he needed to go ahead and die! When his friends came to visit him, they did not recognize him. For seven days and nights, they just sat there without saying a word (Job 2). However, Job knew the long-suffering would have to come to an end. He said, "All the days of my appointed time will I wait, till my change come" (Job 14:14, KJV). When the suffering did stop, Job's latter days were greater than his former.

> *It is written*: "After Job had prayed for his friends, the Lord restored his fortunes and gave him twice as much as he had before" (Job 42:10, NIV).

> "The Lord blessed the latter part of Job's life more than the former part" (Job 42:12, NIV).

The Lord knows who His faithful, upright servants are. He also knows which of us will break under pressure. He will not put any more on us than we can bear. He knows us better than we know ourselves.

> *It is written*: "No temptation[a] has overtaken you except what is common to mankind. And God is faithful; He will not let you be tempted[b] beyond what you can bear. But when you are tempted,[c] He will also provide a way out so that you can endure it" (1 Corinthians 10:13, NIV).

We must also keep in mind that the Lord has suffered long for us. He has been so patient with us, forgiving our sins over and over. We fall, He picks us back up. We fall again and again. He picks us back up, dusts us off, and continues to love us. Over, and over He has shown us love and kindness when we know we do not deserve it. We should be willing to go through for His namesake. No matter how long it takes. It should be all for His glory. We suffer with Him; we reign with Him.

Lord, help us not to complain about our long-suffered trials. We know this is Your story, and You shall get the glory out of our lives. Help us to silence the murmuring and complaining and go through our trials with a smile on our faces and praise in our mouths. Thank You, Lord, for counting us worthy to go through for Your namesake in Jesus' name. Amen.

> *It is written*: "It is good for me that I have been afflicted; that I might learn Thy statutes" (Psalm 119:71, KJV).

> *It is written*: "Many are the afflictions of the righteous: but the Lord delivereth him out of them all" (Psalm 34:19, KJV).

> *It is written*: "And we know that all things work together for good to them that love God, to them who are the called according to His purpose" (Romans 8:28, KJV).

If we find ourselves in uncomfortable situations for a long period of time, we should:

o Thank the Lord for counting us worthy to go *through* it.
o Wait for our *appointed time* to be released from the trial.
o *Do not* complain under any circumstances.
o Speak the Word of God *only*.
o Pray for *others* while we are going through.
o Visualize ourselves *already* out.
o Praise Him in *advance* for releasing us from the trial with a greater latter than our former.

Gentleness

"Be completely humble and gentle; be patient, bearing with one another in love" (Ephesians 4:2, NIV).

Gentleness is a definite necessity in the body of Christ. The unbelievers can see if we are sincere with them. Some of us will portray the role of a gentile believer in the midst of certain members, but as soon as heads are turned, those gentle spirits turn into vipers. It is imperative to be gentle towards one another. We do not know what fragile condition our siblings in Christ might be.

There are more unstable believers in the body of Christ than they should be; however, that is not a reason for us to look away or write those believers off as "drama" members. If that member is coming to church or showing a willingness to want Jesus just a little, we are supposed to be there for them. Sometimes we may have to be gentler. People are rejected over and over by the world. The last thing an individual needs is to come to church seeking change, and we, as the body of Christ, mishandle them. Church hurt is the worst feeling anyone could have. Some people may feel that they can receive better treatment in the world than in the church.

> Jesus said, "If anyone causes one of these little ones—those who believe in Me—to stumble, it would be better for them to have a large millstone hung around their neck and to be drowned in the depths of the sea" (Matthew 18:6, NIV).

Sometimes the members will not attempt to show any type of love or affection towards other members. The members will sit right in the church day in and year out, roll their eyes, walk by other members, will not speak, or when the member does speak, the tone sounds like the member does not want to be bothered. Gentleness goes a long way in the body of Christ. We would be surprised at how far a soft-spoken voice or hug may go with a fragile soul.

> *It is written*: "A gentle answer turns away wrath; but a harsh word stirs up anger" (Proverbs 15:1, NIV).

Goodness

> "Therefore, as we have opportunity, let us do good to all people, especially to those who belong to the family of believers" (Galatians 6:10, NIV).

We, as the body of Christ, will never gain from mistreating a member. At times we may go through the motions of church hurt. Someone may have hurt our feelings, and we get up and leave the church. Truth be told, the church has gotten to the point of we have to walk on pins and needles around other believers because we are so touchy. If someone reaches out to us in love to address some mess, we are waddling, and the first thing we will say is we are being judged or condemned. When 99.99 percent of the time, it is just the Holy Spirit convicting and compelling us to change. We call what is evil good and what is good evil. Some of us reject the truth and yield to simple lies. Some of us mistreat our siblings in Christ and expect royal treatment from everyone. We want members to bow down to us, or we will have a tantrum. The devil is a liar. It is a lot of undercover devils in the body. And some of us cater to them. We entertain and house them, but when a member is concerned about a soul, no one else is saying how the devil is comfortable in that member's body; the individual does not play with the devil, who is now the outcast. Some of us would rather hold on to our demons and twist the truth about the members that love us enough to do something about the devil holding us bound.

Treating our siblings in Christ as outcasts because we can see those demons that are being hidden in the body is not healthy. I love you enough to tell you the truth, pray for you and cast that devil out. I really believe that we are one body, one Christ, and excuse me, but we do not have room for devils in our body! We should not lie to one another to prevent from hurting feelings. I rather hurt you for a moment with the truth than sit up and keep feeding you lies. I am being good to my siblings by telling the truth with no sugar-water.

> *It is written*: "And ye shall know the truth, and the truth shall make you free" (John 8:32, KJV).

Telling our siblings the truth and showing agape love is good. We should never lie to one another or try to manipulate each other. That is not the DNA of the Lord Almighty. We should treat one another how we want to be treated. Amen.

Faith

> "For I say, through the grace given unto me, to every man that is among you, not to think of himself more highly than he ought to think; but to think soberly, according as God hath dealt to every man the measure of faith" (Romans 12:3, KJV).

Meekness

> "Blessed are the meek: for they shall inherit the earth" (Matthew 5:5, KJV).

> "We then that are strong ought to bear the infirmities of the weak, and not to please ourselves" (Romans 15:1, KJV).

Temperance

> "For the grace of God has appeared that offers salvation to all people. It teaches us to say 'No' to ungodliness and worldly passions, and to live self-controlled, upright and godly lives in this present age" (Titus 2:11-12, NIV).

The Help

The Help

When I was putting the puzzle together by myself, there were more times than many I was getting frustrated about the pieces not coming together. I was progressing, but very slowly. One day my daughter came over with her children, and my granddaughter wanted to help put the puzzle together. Her mom grabbed a few pieces and began to put them together as I was trying to nicely say I did not want their help because I was scared they would lose pieces to the puzzle I worked diligently on. My daughter went on giving me the credentials of her and my granddaughter concerning puzzle fixing. I allowed them to help me, but I was still feeling funny about it. I was watching just about their every move.

When I started out working on the assignment by myself, that is how I preferred, but when I saw how my daughter and granddaughter were helping speed up the process, I saw the help a whole different way. My granddaughter was good. She was connecting pieces faster than me. My daughter helped as well. She fixed a huge portion of the puzzle.

There were times my daughter would come to my house and get the puzzle from me and sit down and work for hours putting pieces together. Sometimes the help that God will send us may be the help we were not expecting to come. I felt because they were younger, they did not know the importance of the task I was doing. The help that they gave, gave me hope that it was possible to complete the puzzle.

However, my granddaughter grew bored with it after the first day. My daughter had misplaced some of the puzzle pieces and other pieces she was working on; she ended up connecting them to the wrong parts of the puzzle. She was getting tired and frustrated with the puzzle until one day, she just decided she no longer wanted to work on it anymore, and she gave it back to me. I appreciated all that she had done, but I was once again stuck working on the puzzle by myself.

Time had passed, and I noticed that pieces to the puzzle were on the floor or in places they had no business being. I told my daughter that was exactly what I feared was going to happen. I felt like it would be useless to put the puzzle together because I had seen too many loose pieces lying around the house. My daughter assured me that all the pieces were there, but I found another and another.

When we are working together on an assignment for the Lord, it is everyone who is connected to the assignment's responsibility to tend to the assignment as it were our own personal assignment. We are not supposed to be nonchalant about ministries God has given to someone else. At the end of the day, it is God's ministry, and He is sitting up high and looking down low, watching how we are helping with someone else's ministry.

Also, the ministries were not given to us for us to work alone. We must learn to trust that God will send in the helpers. The ones that do not mind being under the visionary. When God gives one person a vision, and they share the vision with the helpers. The helpers' job is to get with the vision and do what is needed to be done to help bring the vision to pass.

> *It is written*: "And the Lord answered me, and said, Write the vision, and make it plain upon tables, that he may run that readeth it" (Habakkuk 2:2, KJV).

> "For the vision is yet for an appointed time, but at the end it shall speak, and not lie: though it tarry, wait for it; because it will surely come, it will not tarry" (Habakkuk 2:3, KJV).

Think about it: When you are on a construction site, the architect has the vision (blueprint) written down, and he shares it with the helpers. The helpers do not go against the vision and try to build what they want. They build according to the plan.

When God gives us visions, they are merely His plans. That is why He tells us to make the vision plain and write it on tables so those who see it will run (Habakkuk 2:2-3). God says for us to write down the plans so the helpers who see them will know what to do, and they will run with it and build.

I rebuke now, in the name of Jesus, the "takeover" helpers...the ones that come in, see what we are doing, and feel like we are not doing a good enough job, or feel like they can do a better job than us. They come in changing *the* plans to their own plans. The devil is a liar. Sit down somewhere; your kind of help is not needed.

There are some good helpers that will come in and help us build according to *the* plan. They come in to perfect the plans. Those are the kind of helpers we need in the body of Christ. Most likely, they are leaders. These members know that what we are doing is for God, and they want to help promote God too. They do not mind working under the visionary because they understand kingdom movement. They also know that the vision came from God, and He sent them in to help kingdom build. The take-over workers just want the glory and attention. Their motives are stinky.

In ministry, there will sometimes be people who will come in and help to a certain extinct and leave. We cannot and should not get upset about it. God already knew they would do it and trust He always has a "ram in the bush." He provides, period. No need to worry or get frustrated when they leave before the work is completed. God got us! He gave us the vision; trust that there is *plenty* of provisions. God provides.

I did not notice offhand that my daughter had misconnected some of the pieces until I was working on a certain section of the puzzle and could not find a piece. I looked closer to the puzzle and noticed there were two pieces out of place on the puzzle, and I had to disconnect the pieces and connect the right one. Because my daughter had gotten frustrated with the puzzle, it caused her to connect some of the wrong pieces together. Sometimes we can be frustrated with a ministry assignment. It may look like things are not connecting as they should, so we may take it upon ourselves and try to connect other members that do not belong to the assignment we are working on. God wants us to take our time and correctly connect each member to His design. We all have a purpose. If what we are working with is frustrating us, maybe we need to step away for a few minutes and pray. Sometimes we can work on something so long to where we get frustrated and end up overlooking the very thing; we need to help the ministry run smoother. Again, if we get frustrated, we should step away for a minute and pray. Ask the Lord to reveal to us what we are not seeing. He will reveal.

Also, we must know when and how long to allow people to help us with ministry. We do not want to give them more than they can handle. When someone is given a position in the ministry God has given us, we must realize that sometimes it may become overwhelming to them, and they will begin to make mistakes. Simple mistakes. We still are to appreciate our help, but at the same time, remember that they are our "help." They are helping us to complete an assignment. God did not give the vision to them. He gave it to us. Amen. We must remember to whom much is given, much is required (Luke 12:48). We should not push off on others what was given to us because they may not have the grace that we have to complete the assignment. If they are willing to help, let them, but do not push the whole thing off on them or expect them to do tons of work. We must remember that the assignment was given to the visionary to complete.

Forcing Pieces

When connecting the puzzle pieces, they must fit the design. They cannot be forced.

When I was working on the puzzle alone and meditating on what I was doing, the pieces were coming together faster, but I noticed there was a portion of the puzzle I could not complete because I could not find the pieces. It was hard for me to move along to the next section without the pieces to the puzzle. So, I began to look carefully at the puzzle and found the error. My daughter had put some pieces together that looked like they belonged together, but they did not.

Those few pieces messed up the whole portion of the puzzle and the portion I was working on because the pieces were in the wrong place. God showed me that about us. We are pieces to the puzzle to the assignment He has given us, but just because we belong to the assignment does not mean we get to go work on another portion of the assignment. We must fit in where we belong, or else we will mess up the parts that belong to someone else.

We may be good at one thing, and we feel we are supposed to be over there working with that one thing, but God may have assigned us to work somewhere else because our strength may be needed in that area.

We should not try to force ourselves in ministry; our gifts will make room for us. Amen.

> *It is written*: "A man's gift maketh room for him, and bringeth him before great men" (Proverbs 18:16, KJV).

Seeing the Manifestation of the Vision

The more I worked on the puzzle, the more I began to see the picture the way it was on the box. Seeing the picture coming together made me want to keep striving to complete the puzzle.

If we are given an assignment to do, and we work on it and work on it, and cannot see it coming together, maybe it was not God that gave us the assignment. When God gives us assignments, He gives us the visual of the assignment, and He equips us with everything we need to complete the assignment.

Today when God gives certain members of His body assignments to do, the member might go to show the other members that God has ordained to work on the assignment as well and tell the members that God said they are a part of the assignment. The members want to get *scuba deep* and say, "Let me pray about it..." pretty much laughing in our faces and telling us in so many words that God did not tell us to do the assignment. Usually, when someone says, "Let me pray about it," 99.99 percent of the time, that is a nice way for them to say *no*. When we go back to ask them what God told them about it...that is the answer they come up with.

Furthermore, there should be some confirmation somewhere in the mist. God will already have laid it on the helpers' hearts to help with the vision. However, these days when the Lord speaks to some members about helping others build, we may say it is not God telling the member that, or we may shut out His voice because we do not want to work under or help someone else in ministry. These days everybody wants to lead...be the chiefs, and no followers...Indians! Everybody wants to open churches or build our own ministries, and many of us have no structure or leadership skills. Many of us are just rebellious children that dropped out of a church because we did not want to sit under authority. Pastor would not give us the position we wanted, so now we left the church to build our own, and God has not told some of us to leave. Now that was not expected to be said, but it is here now, and I am unapologetic about saying it because it is the truth.

Too many Jezebel/controlling spirits have risen and trying to take over the body of Christ. Many of us do not want to submit to authority, so we are coming up with our cheesy little ministries, and we are taxing the saints to keep them open, selling all kinds of things in the name of the Lord. Well, Jesus went in then and flipped over tables, and He is about to do it again. We (body of Christ) must get back on one accord with one another and stop this dividing the churches and strife, competition, unforgiveness, and hate. It needs to stop now! We are giving too much room for the devil to come in.

Now correct me if I am wrong. God is not going to speak two separate things to two individuals about an assignment. Meaning, if God told me that you are a part of the assignment, He is not going to go and tell you that you are not. Somebody is lying on God.

If we trust God in one another and if someone comes to us saying they have an assignment from on High and we are included, we are not supposed to say, "Let me pray about it," but instead say that we are glad to support the cause. When we do that, whatever we may have going on that may stand in the way of us helping with the assignment. God will give grace and favor on our behalf.

I remember once the Lord told me to bless this sister with a new television set. He had been dealing with me about watching too much TV, so He laid it on my heart not to sale it but to give it away to a sister who had four children. When I called the sister to tell her I had to get rid of the new TV, she did not answer her phone. I called her a few times and left messages and got no returned answer. Later, the Lord sent another sister by my house, and He told me to give the television to her. When I went to church later that week, the sister told me, "God told me to not answer your calls." I just laughed at this memory because it was many years ago when this happened, and I did not have the wisdom then that I have now. I must say that it was not God Almighty who told her not to answer my calls. I told her, "Well, God told me to bless you with a new television," and all she could do was shake her head and still confess that the Lord told her not to answer the phone, but she sure needed the television set for her children because the one they had was old and about to go out. She missed out on her blessing because she would not answer the phone.

God is leading me to say this right now. Some of us need to stop ignoring phone calls because we do not want to talk to an individual. We say we want to work ministry but to a certain extinct. We want a "Burger King" ministry. Have it our way. I speak to myself concerning this as well because I do not know how many times I have ignored calls from people because I felt like they were time wasters, ones that like to talk a lot and usually not talking about anything, or people that I had hidden agendas about, people that may have hurt me and we never really talked about how they hurt me, and we became okay once again with each other, but I put a wall up to make sure they do not try me again. I made sure not to answer their calls or get involved with them like that again. First time, shame on them, second time, shame on me, I thought. Sometimes we get too emotional about people and situations, and we allow our emotions to paint a different picture to the puzzle. We begin to see things differently. Our emotions can cloud our vision. I pray that we see past the pain and see the real picture in Jesus' name. It is not about us. Amen.

Also, some of us will get jealous when God gives someone else an assignment we want to do, and we would rather sit up and watch the member struggle with the assignment than step in as loving siblings should and help. It is sad that the body of Christ will sit up and watch other members fall and say, "Um-hum, told you he could not" or "she would not."

> *It is written*: "Let them be desolate for a reward of their shame that say unto me, Aha, aha" (Psalm 40:15).

We, as the body of Christ, better be careful of how we treat our siblings. God is not pleased. Stop wishing failure on one another. It is like us wanting God to fail because He is the One handing out the assignments. We are building for Him. Why would we want someone else in the body to stumble and fall? God said His people perish for lack of knowledge (Hosea 4:1). Wanting another member of the body to fail demonstrates our ignorance. While we are sitting around laughing at our siblings stumbling, the devil is sitting around laughing at us because we cannot seem to stop operating in division while the devil and his army are unifying to destroy us. Come on, body of Christ, we need to do better than what we are doing.

Some of us will see the pieces coming together after we have left the visionary hanging, then we want to come back and help in the end and then expect the recognition as if we have been there helping all along. We should not get bitter or discouraged when these types of members show up later. Maybe God allowed the members to step away because of unbelief. Remember, He did say that without faith, it is impossible to please Him. Unbelief is contagious. If it is around too long, it will contaminate other faith walkers. So, it must be cast out in the name of Jesus.

Personally, I always say the ones that come in the end are relatives of Apostle Thomas. Apostle Thomas walked with Jesus for three years, and his name is remembered in the Bible for being a doubter. He said, "Except I shall see in His hands the print of the nails, and put my finger into the print of the nails, and thrust my hand into His side, I will not believe" (John 20:25, KJV).

Some people are like that; they must see it first before they believe it. Jesus said, "Because you have seen me, you have believed; blessed are those who have not seen and yet have believed"(John 20:29, NIV). Being a visionary, I count it a privilege and honor to be able to visualize what the Lord is saying. Being able to see the picture before it is developed is a true gift we should not take for granted. If we can see the picture of His divine design coming together, we must believe Him and keep building.

Noah was a visionary. He did not have any natural plans to build an ark to hold tons of animals and stand up against the storm that came and destroyed mankind. God had to show him what that ark looked like. He had to show him all he needed to build it strong. There is no possible way Noah could have built without a vision. There is no possible way none of us can build without a vision. Not naturally or spiritually. Once we see the picture, it will encourage us to build. That is if we have faith in Him. Amen.

Losing Interest

The more I worked on the puzzle, the more I begin to feel like I would never finish it because I felt like my daughter had lost some pieces to it; I would have been very disappointed if I went all the way to the end and pieces were missing. It had come to the point that I was so frustrated I could no longer see what pieces connected anymore. The pieces began to get harder and harder to connect. After a few weeks of trying and trying to fit the pieces together and was unsuccessful, I really felt in my heart the pieces were missing. That is why I was not able to connect them as well as I had been doing before.

I lost interest in working on the puzzle, and I found it harder to make myself do it. I had ministry coming up. I was at the end of my class, and it was very intense. I was going through some personal issues, and I just did not feel like dealing with a jigsaw puzzle. Besides, there was nothing else God has spoken to me about it. I worked on it less and less. And I was so close to finishing it. As close as I was to the end, I was surprised at how I was losing interest in putting it together.

The Lord showed me how some of us work on things in the ministry for long periods of time, and we lose our spark. We may get tired of going through the persecutions and trials for the ministry. It *looks* like no one really cares anyway. We may suffer and go through for someone else while they are sitting up living the good life and unappreciative about what we are going through for them. But we cannot get weary about it. We must remember that we are not doing it for ourselves, but we are doing it for the Lord.

Sometimes God will remove people and things from our lives to help us to remember what we are supposed to be focusing on. Sometimes we lose interest in things because we find other things to occupy our time. How many of us know that God is a jealous God, and when He gives us something to do, we are supposed to do it? Sometimes He will let us slide and go through the motion for a little bit, but when we tend to stray too far away, He sure knows how to grasp our attention and bring us back in to complete our assignment.

Putting It Back in the Box

In the last section, I spoke about how I began to lose interest in the puzzle and thought so many times about quitting. After the puzzle sat on the table for about a month and I found other things to do. I did quit working on it, and I put the "unsolved" pieces back in the box and put the puzzle in my room on the dresser. I said I would start on it again later. I will be honest, later never came. The puzzle sat on my dresser in my room for months. I did not go in my room that much, but when I did, it was briefly. After a while, I had noticed how I began to pile things on top of the fixed portion of the puzzle. I had placed mail, books, magazines, lotion, and hats on top of the puzzle. There it lay buried under all that stuff, and I did not think anything else about it. The puzzle box ended up in my junk drawer for later.

I had gone to visit my sister in Christ that also had an assignment to complete a jigsaw puzzle. Hers was so intense; she had two puzzles in one to assemble. The first time I visited her, I saw the puzzle on the table and where she had attempted to put a few pieces together. I sat at her table while I was there and connected some pieces for her. The next time I went to visit her, some months later, the puzzle was still on the table in the same spot, but she had a box sitting on top of it and other things around it.

The Lord showed me recently how we have visions, ministries, talents that we give birth to and abandon. We may work on them to a certain extent; then, we lose interest in them. We may find something else that is more exciting to do, and we focus on doing those things for a while until we get tired of them too. And it goes on and on. The next thing we know, we have so many talents, gifts, ministries started and not finished. God showed me that when we stop, we are putting the "talent," "gift," "ministry" back in the box. We say we will work on it later; we just do not really have time for it now. Truth be told, we make time for what we want to make time for. We just get bored with doing things. I am a writer. I love writing, but sometimes I just did not feel like writing because I wanted to watch television or I wanted to be on social media. I felt like I did not have the money to publish what I wrote, so why waste my time writing. It was not like someone would ever get a chance to read what I wrote...unless it was on social media, I thought to myself. I began spending just about *all my time* online writing my thoughts, building an audience of listeners, but deep down inside, I still was not satisfied. There was more. I could feel it, but I could not do anything because I had put my writing talent back in the box. I could not write the things I write in books on social media. People want to read something short. They want a quick fix, and I am not a short, quick-fix writer. I like to write about the things God shows me and go deeper with them, hear what it is He is trying to show me, and I could not write that online.

Many years ago, it was prophesied to me that I was a book writer, and the books written would be in major bookstores. I heard it, and I attempted to write a book many years ago and self-publish it. I ended up with a whole bunch of books with grammar and spelling errors. The book never made it past a selected people in my city. It was like the puzzle; I was given an assignment, I worked on it, got tired of doing it because it did not look like it was going anywhere, so I put it back in the box and began working on other things.

Right now, I have a book I started writing almost twenty years ago sitting on top of my closet, collecting dust. I have been saying for years I am going to finish the book and never have. Because the first book was not a success, I stopped working on the second one...a book about my life. It has been sitting on top of my closet unfinished since 2002. Twenty years ago, we did not have laptops; we had word processors and typewriters, and that book is written in ink and typewriting format, but I hear the Lord telling me the word "upgrade."

God is going to give many of you reading this book an *upgrade.* The things that you have placed back in the box and no longer had interest in. I see God "blowing the dust off," so you will be able to see the picture/vision again. He is going to give you grace to restart it and, this time, finish it in the name of Jesus. Amen, boom impartation!

When I covered up that puzzle and put away the pieces in the box, they were no longer in my sight. When we do not have a vision of what needs to be done, we cannot work on it. God is giving a lot of us our visions back. And may we not lose them again. Amen.

Throwing Away

One day while sweeping, I found more pieces to the puzzle I was working on and went ahead and decided I no longer had to beat myself up or feel convicted about not completing the puzzle I had pushed to the side. As I continued to clean my room, I noticed that there were too many loose pieces lying around. I do not know what happened and how all those pieces ended up everywhere. I took it upon myself to sweep up the loose pieces and disposed of them and the puzzle. Well, that was it. I was finally free from completing the puzzle. That is what I thought at the time! I did not have to worry anymore about feeling convicted for not completing the assignment.

When the Lord spoke to me and told me to write this book, He already knew that I would not complete the puzzle. How many of us know that God knows us better than we know ourselves? He told me not to sugarcoat anything about what I learned from putting the puzzle together, and that included telling on myself. God can be funny sometimes. The Lord used my own hands to chastise me and to help me to see my faults in His divine design. Although I was not able to finish assembling the puzzle, He did use the puzzle to teach me so many things that He also wanted me to share with those who happen to come across this book and read it. Know that it is not by chance you are reading this, but it is His will.

God has revealed more to me *after* the fact that He has while I was putting it together. I am so glad I was obedient and bought the puzzle. Who would have thought that a dollar puzzle would have so much substance? If I would have brought the candy bar, instead, I would still be walking around here asking Him why this and why that.

God showed me when I ended up throwing the puzzle away how it was already in His plan for me to do. Had I finished the puzzle, I would not have gotten the revelation from me not finishing it. It was all part of His plan for me not to finish the puzzle.

Next, what He taught me from throwing the puzzle away was how I was feeling relieved. I had a good justification why I did not have to finish something I had been putting off for months that He told me to do. I *finally* found a way out. He gave me a way of escape at that time. My excuse was, I lost the pieces.

God showed me that when He tells us to do something we really do not want to do, we find the smallest things to justify why we cannot do it, but when there is something that we want to do; we go above, beyond, through dungeons, turn cheetah flips and walk tight ropes to do what we want to do.

Sometimes there are members we do not want to connect with, the member may do something "petty" or "minor," and we make a big deal out of it to justify why we cannot connect. It is time out for the isms and schisms. We all fall short of His glory, and siblings do argue with one another, but the bond that siblings have cannot be broken. We need to act like siblings and stop running around here getting angry about petty things that keep us from kingdom building. That is all the trick of the enemy to hinder us and keep us divided. Remember, united we stand, and divided we fall.

Imagine a puzzle split in half…it will never be what it was created to be by being split. Being split was not the purpose. Its purpose was to be completed as a whole. We keep saying we are one body and one Christ, so why do we keep separating with one another and walking in division? *Selah!*

We cannot just decide to work on God's divine design when we want to. We cannot work on it until we decide we are tired of it. He said, "Do not get weary in well-doing; we will reap if we faint not." We cannot get tired and put our pieces…our gifts back in the box.

Remember what the Lord said about hiding our talents (Matthew 25:14-30). We cannot just cut people out of the plan and throw them away. The first thing many of us say is, "Only God can judge me," but we are the first to judge one another and quit on each other.

The body of Christ has it worse than the people of the world because it is entirely too much hate, bitterness, and unforgiveness amongst us. There is too much comparing and competing with one another and not enough working together and completing the Master's plan with one another. God is not pleased. I just heard the Lord say, "What if I decide to throw the plan away? You are all a piece of My divine design. What if I get tired of each of you and decide to start another plan and just throw you away? Do not think I will not do it. Remember Noah and the Ark." My God, have mercy on us. Lord, help us to get it right in Jesus' name. Amen.

Five years have passed since my jigsaw puzzle assignment. The Lord had shown me then, but I was in denial about being a quitter. He said He will put no more on us than we can bear, and if it is too much, He will give us a way to escape. He had to work with me for a while about completing things He gave me to start. I had to learn how to finish things. I have another jigsaw puzzle assignment to complete after the completion of the publication of this book.

Believe me when I say, He did not let me get away with not finishing that puzzle. He turned this book into a puzzle itself. I had to work long hours piecing this book together. I remember at one time, I had to print out the manuscript so I could write on the pages. After seeing how I crossed out this, circled that, rectangle here and there, I realized from the manuscript God was working that patience in me and frustration out of me. He was still getting the glory. I may have thrown away the physical puzzle, but He knew I would not throw away the manuscript. He made me assemble this book. I wanted to quit, but I knew I could not. I was already in the publishing process, and the kingdom finances had already been supplied to publish this book. I had no choice in the matter but to complete this assignment.

I had not realized how many things I have started and quit throughout the course of my life. Do not get it twisted; I have finished a lot of assignments, but God wanted to strengthen me in this area. I decree I am a finisher. I do not abort or abandon any assignment given to me by God in Jesus' name, amen. I am telling myself: my God has been so good to me. I should have been dead and gone, but He still shows His everlasting love towards me. Trust when I say He is no respecter of persons. If He did it for me, He will do it for you. Amen.

A Different Perspective

A Different Perspective

Five years have passed since the time of my jigsaw puzzle assembling assignment. The Lord has enhanced my knowledge concerning the assignment and compelled me to add what else I have learned from the assignment to this book.

> So God created man in His own image, in the image of God created He Him; male and female created He them. And God blessed them, and God said unto them, Be fruitful, and multiply, and replenish the earth, and subdue it: and have dominion over the fish of the sea, and over the fowl of the air, and over every living thing that moveth upon the earth.
>
> Genesis 1:27-28 (KJV)

The Employer

How many of us know that everything has a purpose? From the beginning of time, the Lord has been handing down assignments to all creation. When He created light, He assigned it to shine in the day, and darkness was assigned to show up at its appointed time. Everything on this earth has an assignment given by our Creator.

> *It is written*: "To everything there is a season, and a time to every purpose under the heaven" (Ecclesiastes 3:1, NIV).

Everything with purpose has an assignment for a certain time. For instance, God assigned winter to be cold, time to move forward one hour in the spring, and back one hour in the fall. Trees have many assignments, one being to provide oxygen to help us breathe.

> *It is written*: "As long as the earth endures, seedtime and harvest, cold and heat, summer and winter, day and night will never cease" (Genesis 8:22, NIV).

He gave everything and every being on the face of this earth assignments. Adam and Eve were the first human beings to receive an assignment from Him. He said, "Be fruitful and multiply" (Genesis 1:28, KJV).

If God assigned the wind to blow and fish to live underwater; there is a reason, a purpose for them; what makes us think that we are excused for our divine assignments? *Selah!*

We all have something we are supposed to be doing for the Lord. He designed it from the beginning of time.

There are consequences given to those of us who do not accept our divine assignments from the Lord. Remember Jesus walking by a fig tree that had no figs, and He cursed it. That fig tree had a divine assignment to bear figs. The tree did not do what it was purposed to do. Its assignment was to bear figs. God had an appointed time for Jesus to connect with the tree and be able to eat from it. The fig tree knew it was assigned to bear figs. That tree just wanted to hang and not do anything. Jesus was hungry; the tree was not able to feed the One that gave it life. It had to go.

> *It is written*: "Early in the morning, as Jesus was on His way back to the city, He was hungry. Seeing a fig tree by the road, He went up to it but found nothing on it except leaves. Then He said to it, 'May you never bear fruit again!' Immediately the tree withered" (Matthew 21:18-19, NIV).

There are members in the body of Christ that the Lord will assign to be over some of the members. We, the body of Christ, have been acting out of line towards those who are in leadership. Some of us do not want to submit to the authority the Lord has given us. The leader might ask a member to do something for the ministry, and the member may reject the assignment because of who it is that is giving the assignment.

Some members try to accept every assignment in the church to prevent other members from gaining access. Some members accept the assignments to be recognized and praised by other members.

> *It is written*: "Whatever you do, work at it with all your heart, as working for the Lord, not for human masters" (Colossians 3:23, NIV).

Mind Battles against Assignments

At times, we might have a difficult assignment given to us by the Lord. Deep down inside, some of us get excited when He chooses us for an assignment. We really want to do it, but it is when we start thinking about how big the assignment is, how difficult it may be, how time-consuming it is, how much it cost, and so forth that causes us to slip into the doubting Thomas/double-minded stage. Some of us allow fear to feed our thoughts, telling us we cannot do it, we are not good enough, we do not have the money, or what will "they" think? What if I fail? The more we begin to think about the who, what, when, where, and how of the assignment, the more we allow our thoughts to become contaminated with impure things that try to stir us away from our divine purpose and plan God has for our lives. The more we entertain thoughts that are not lining up with His Word, the more they begin to stink. They are unclean thoughts. Yes, our thoughts can be stinky! Anything that is not clean normally has an odor to it. We do not want to be a funky smell to God's nostrils. Every time we think opposite of what He says about us is like us intentionally throwing skunk fumes in His face.

The Lord is not going to give us anything that will harm us. Whatever He gives us is good. We should not have to suspect or inspect anything in our thoughts of what He gives us.

> Jesus said, "Which of you, if your son asks for bread, will give him a stone? Or if he asks for a fish, will give him a snake? If you, then, though you are evil, know how to give good gifts to your children, how much more will your Father in heaven give good gifts to those who ask Him!" (Matthew 7:9-11, NIV).

> *It is written*: "For I know the thoughts that I think toward you, saith the Lord, thoughts of peace, and not of evil, to give you an expected end" (Jeremiah 29:11, KJV).

> *It is written*: "For My thoughts are not your thoughts, neither are your ways My ways, saith the Lord. For as the heavens are higher

than the earth, so are My ways higher than your ways, and My thoughts than your thoughts" (Isaiah 55:8-9, KJV).

He will not send us anywhere to be ambushed. Every assignment He gives us is already designated. It is all in His plan. We have an expected end. That is why He tells us to rejoice and be glad every day, walk by faith and not by sight, trust in Him with all our hearts, and not lean to our own understanding because He knows every single thing that is going to happen and when it is going to happen. It is all a part of His plan. He wants us to do parts that He has assigned to us in His plan from the beginning of time. We need to captivate those impure thoughts that try to override His Word and bring them into the obedience of Christ. Our thoughts must line up with His Word.

It is written: "Finally, brothers and sisters, whatever is true, whatever is noble, whatever is right, whatever is pure, whatever is lovely, whatever is admirable—if anything is excellent or praiseworthy— think about such things" (Philippians 4:8, NIV).

It is written: "Set your minds on things above, not on earthly things. For you died, and your life is now hidden with Christ in God. When Christ, who is your[a] life, appears, then you also will appear with Him in glory" (Colossians 3:2-4, NIV).

It is written: "For God hath not given us the spirit of fear; but of power, and of love, and of a sound mind" (2 Timothy 1:7, KJV).

It is written: "Trust in the Lord with all thine heart; and lean not unto thine own understanding. In all thy ways acknowledge Him, and He shall direct thy paths" (Proverbs 3:5-6, KJV).

Concerning Leadership

"Then I will give you shepherds after My own heart, who will lead you with knowledge and understanding" (Jeremiah 3:15, NIV).

It is imperative to know who we are destined to sit under in leadership. To be strong kingdom people, we must eat healthily. We are living in a time where there are more "sugar water" ministries in the land than sound doctrine. Some leaders focus more on the number of members than the condition of the souls. Many leaders today are not sent by God. There are a lot of motivational speakers claiming to be ministers of God. Many preach to satisfy flesh and the pocket. If anyone in leadership is not preaching salvation of Jesus Christ, healing, repentance, holiness, deliverance...the unadulterated truth of the Gospel of Jesus Christ, God did not send them. God did not call us to be leaders to sugar-coat or water down His Word. He did not send His chosen vessels to scratch itching ears. He sent us to preach the truth, His sound doctrine to set captives free. We are not to add or take away from His Word, making it a null effect. Jesus said if we love Him, feed His sheep, not poison them!

> *It is written*: "So when they had dined, Jesus saith to Simon Peter, Simon, son of Jonas, lovest thou Me more than these? He saith unto Him, Yea, Lord; thou knowest that I love Thee. He saith unto him, Feed My lambs. He saith to him again the second time, Simon, son of Jonas, lovest thou Me? He saith unto Him, Yea, Lord; thou knowest that I love Thee. He saith unto him, Feed My sheep. He saith unto him the third time, Simon, son of Jonas, lovest thou Me? Peter was grieved because He said unto him the third time, Lovest thou Me? And he said unto Him, Lord, thou knowest all things; thou knowest that I love Thee. Jesus saith unto him, Feed My sheep" (John 21:15-17, KJV).

Every time we preach lies, we are poisoning the Lord's sheep, and we will have to give an account.

Imagine this: You leave your children for three days with someone that you trust will take good care of them. While you are away, all that trusted person gave your children to eat was sweets and candy. For three days and nights, your children feasted on junk foods. Your children become sick because of what someone you trusted has fed them. How would that make you feel? *Selah!*

How do we think the Lord feels about us feeding His sheep unhealthy spiritual foods, poisoning the body? Jesus asked Peter three times if he loved Him. He was trying to get it in Peter's mind that He was going away, and He trusted Peter, the rock, to feed His sheep. Peter needed to tend to His sheep as though He was still there in the flesh.

The Lord is telling the body of Christ as a whole, starting from leadership, to feed His sheep. If we could literally see Jesus in the flesh the same way His disciples did, would we really feed His sheep anything other than His true unadulterated Word? I do not think so. We are to treat the members of the body of Christ as though He is right in front of us. Truth be told, He is there watching. We just cannot see Him. Again, the Lord says, feed His sheep the truth, not poison.

> *It is written*: "For the word of God is alive and active. Sharper than any double-edged sword, it penetrates even to dividing soul and spirit, joints and marrow; it judges the thoughts and attitudes of the heart" (Hebrews 4:12, NIV).

Some members are bound because some of us that are in leadership do not want to preach the truth.

> *It is written*: "And ye shall know the truth, and the truth shall make you free" (John 8:32, KJV).

Preaching the truth heals, delivers, sets captives free. For those members in leadership who do not desire to help set the captives free by preaching God's unadulterated truth may need to take a seat for a couple of seasons and allow the Lord to deliver. The Lord does not play about His sheep.

Sometimes we, as the body of Christ, will sit under members to support ministries when God did not tell us to sit under that one leader. Sitting under wrong leadership can bring stagnation to our growth. Sometimes we may outgrow certain ministries, and the Lord may send us somewhere else to be nurtured so we can grow further. However, some leaders cannot accept it when the time comes for the members to move along. Some leaders will order the members to not associate with the member who left the church.

Some leaders will fill the members' thoughts with negativity about the members who leave the church. Most think that when a member leaves the church, they have backslid. Some members may have backslidden, but it is not for us, as the body of Christ, to gossip and spread rumors about that member. We are to pray, reach out to the member, and continue to show love. Ministries that have gossiping pastors, or those in leadership, are ministries with holes. God cannot pour into cracked vessels.

> *It is written*: "A gossip betrays a confidence, but a trustworthy person keeps a secret" (Proverbs 11:13, NIV).

> *It is written*: "He that goeth about as a talebearer revealeth secrets: therefore meddle not with him that flattereth with his lips" (Proverbs 20:19, KJV).

If we cannot share what is troubling us to our leaders without having to worry if it will be shared with other church members or preached about on Sunday morning, who else can we turn to in confidentiality? That is why a lot of members are going through trials alone because we do not know who we can trust to really pray with us without talebearing. Leaders saying, "Let us pray for Sister Ellen; she is having problems with this or that" is also a form of gossip. If leaders ask members to pray for the one in need of prayer, that is all we need to say unless the member makes a specific request to all. Otherwise, the Holy Spirit will lead the intercessors as what to pray for. The holes must be sealed in Jesus' name.

We must tame our tongues and guard our ears. Individuals in leadership it is not godly to slander the sheep's names, especially when the time has come to leave the ministry. We are to send the members out with our blessings with assuring that we are here when needed.

Instructions

> "Remind the people to be subject to rulers and authorities, to be obedient, to be ready to do whatever is good" (Titus 3:1, NIV).

Every assignment given to us comes with instructions. It is imperative to know what we are supposed to do once we have been given an assignment.

Everyone that has a role in the assignment must communicate with one another while working on the assignment. A lot of assignments fail due to not following the instructions and having poor communication amongst the workers.

Imagine this: You order a king-size bedroom set from a furniture store online. When the mailman delivers your package, you find out that the whole set needs to be assembled. When you look at the picture on the box, you may think that it is not so bad; you can do it. Once you open the boxes and pull out all the material, you realize that it is a bit more complicated. You ask your siblings to help you assemble the set. They all agree. You glimpse at the instructions and decide that they are too long to read or too complicated. You all start assembling the set by looking at the picture on the boxes. You all are putting short screws where long screws go. You are assembling some of the pieces backward. You cannot figure out where the piece goes. One of your siblings has a screw you need, but you do not know it. You are all busy trying to figure out how to assemble the bedroom set. Some of the pieces fit, and some do not. There is no communication between you and your siblings because you are all occupied with trying to figure out something on your own when you all should have sat down and read the instructions first. You all may have been in the same workspace, but you were not working together. There was no communication about what you were trying to assemble on your own. Everybody was in their own little world working on the assignment. That is not teamwork. Sorry, but not sorry! *Selah!*

As kingdom builders, we should be able to receive instructions without any contention between a member and the one giving the instructions. Once we receive our instructions, we should follow them. It is not meant for a member to alter the instructions. If a member has ideas to help better the assignment without completely deviating away from the plan and would like to share the ideas with the team, that should be fine.

However, if that member does not share the ideas with the individual that has been placed over the assignment and tries to implement the ideas, tries to talk the team into overthrowing the original plan, that member is out of order. That is like having a CEO hand out instructions to do something prosperous and purposeful, and an employee decides they have a better plan they want to execute. They tell all the other employees but refuse to mention it to the CEO. If we are not going to behave in that manner when on our natural jobs, then we should not behave in that manner when working for the Lord. *Selah!*

How many times do we say that God is our Boss/Employer and He is the only One we answer to? But we still do not answer to Him when He gives us an assignment. Let the truth be told. When we are on our natural jobs, and if our employer gives us an assignment that we refuse to produce the work, the employer has an option to discipline us according to our actions, or they have the option to terminate us for insubordination.

The Lord has just instructed me to break down the word "insubordination." I am sure many of us know what the word means, but I must obey Him.

Insubordination: "The act of willfully disobeying an order of one's superior, being disobedient to authority."[1] "Disrespect shown to higher-ups in the form of vulgar or mocking language. Directly

---

[1]   http://www.dictionary.com.

questioning or mocking management decisions."[2] When the employee has a difference of opinion with the manager and confronts the manager in front of everyone else on the team. Insubordination is determined when an individual is given an assignment, understands the assignment, but refuses to do the assignment.

Gross insubordination is a bit more intense. Individuals that are accused of gross insubordination are usually terminated on the spot. Theft, fraud, dishonesty, bullying, refusal to wear personal protective equipment, deliberately damaging property, using or selling drugs, horseplay, sexual harassment, and threats are some of the forms of gross insubordination.

The natural definitions were written to show some of us how we have been operating in spiritual insubordination. Again, what the Lord reveals naturally, He will also reveal the spiritual. Some of us are willfully disobeying those who have authority over us. Some of us are disrespectful to our leaders and elders. We might make fun of what our leaders are doing. They might have an event, and only a few people show up. Some of us get in our little groups to gossip and criticize our leaders. Some of us are disrespectful to those who are in authority over us. We attempt to publicly embarrass them, or when we are in front of certain members, we act differently. Some of us turn into spiritual bullies when we are with other members. God sees it all. This is a warning to many of us to clean it up. Some of us are being disciplined right now by the Lord and do not understand why we are going through it. It may be because of disrespecting and disobeying our leaders.

> *It is written*: "Obey them that have the rule over you, and submit yourselves: for they watch for your souls, as they that must give account, that they may do it with joy, and not with grief: for that is unprofitable for you" (Hebrews 13:17, KJV).

---

[2]   http://www.wikipedia.com

It is written: "Let everyone be subject to the governing authorities, for there is no authority except that which God has established. The authorities that exist have been established by God. Consequently, whoever rebels against the authority is rebelling against what God has instituted, and those who do so will bring judgment on themselves. For rulers hold no terror for those who do right, but for those who do wrong. Do you want to be free from fear of the one in authority? Then do what is right and you will be commended. For the one in authority is God's servant for your good. But if you do wrong, be afraid, for rulers do not bear the sword for no reason. They are God's servants, agents of wrath to bring punishment on the wrongdoer. Therefore, it is necessary to submit to the authorities, not only because of possible punishment but also as a matter of conscience" (Romans 13:1-5, NIV).

Spiritual Gross Insubordination

Some of us are in the church stealing money from the collection plates. Some of us are not being honest about the donations that are coming in the ministries. Some of us are having fundraisers in the name of Jesus but keeping the money for ourselves. Some of us are taking out loans in the ministry name but spending the funds in our own households. Some of us are receiving increases in our finances but not paying our tithes and offering. Some of us are paying our tithes after we buy what we want, and then we short-change God on His ten percent. Some of us are ordaining and licensing ourselves and opening churches and ministries God did not approve of. Some of us are creating titles for ourselves that are not even mentioned in the Bible. Some of us are giving ourselves titles and positions that were not authorized by God. Some of us are using our God-given titles to get what our flesh wants.

Some of us are spiritual bullies. We, the body of Christ, talk down on other members. We hold grudges against our siblings. Some of us constantly pick on our siblings, pushing them out of the church. Some of us deliberately strike to damage God's property. Some of us are playing around with witchcraft. Some of us are mixing love potions, money potions, consuming alcohol, using drugs, selling drugs, selling, and misusing prescription drugs. Some of us are turning to psychics, card readers, wizards. Some of us are physically aggressive and secretly abusing our spouses. Some of us refuse to use our spiritual protection, our sword of the Spirit, the Word of God. The Lord says many of us have been warned. Some of us may have stopped but later picked it back up, and it is now more intense than before.

> *It is written*: "When an impure spirit comes out of a person, it goes through arid places seeking rest and does not find it. Then it says, 'I will return to the house I left.' When it arrives, it finds the house unoccupied, swept clean and put in order. Then it goes and takes with it seven other spirits more wicked than itself, and they go in and live there. And the final condition of that person is worse than the first" (Matthew 12:43-45, NIV).

This is a strong warning for my siblings in Christ that are involved in these wrongdoings. The Lord is about to cut you off. Repent! Please.

> *It is written*: "If we say that we have no sin, we deceive ourselves, and the truth is not in us. If we confess our sins, He is faithful and just to forgive us our sins, and to cleanse us from all unrighteousness. If we say that we have not sinned, we make Him a liar, and His word is not in us" (1 John 1:8-10, KJV).

> *It is written*: "Whoever remains stiff-necked after many rebukes will suddenly be destroyed—without remedy" (Proverbs 29:1, NIV).

> *It is written*: "Therefore everyone who hears these words of Mine and puts them into practice is like a wise man who built his house on the rock. The rain came down, the streams rose, and the winds blew and beat against that house; yet it did not fall, because it had its foundation on the rock. But everyone who hears these words of Mine and does not put them into practice is like a foolish man who built his house on sand. The rain came down, the streams rose, and the winds blew and beat against that house, and it fell with a great crash" (Matthew 7:24-27, NIV).

The Due Date

When we are given an assignment, we are also given the location where we will be working on the assignment. We will be given a due date and the supplies that we need by the employer to work on the assignment.

When the Lord told me over five years ago to buy a jigsaw puzzle and assemble it, I knew that the place where I would be assembling it would be at home in my living room. At the time, I did not know that I had an expected due date to finish assembling the puzzle. As time passed, I had learned that He wanted me to write a book about what He was going to show me in the jigsaw puzzle. Years ago, I wrote this book, and it has been stored on my laptop unpublished. I said, "Well, I did write the book." Here it is five years later, bit by bit, I could see Him leading me back to doing something with this book. I would go in my closet and see one of the rough draft self-publishing versions of the book. I would toss it to the side, and a few months later, it would pop up again. Once, it popped up in one of my photo memories. Then, I would start seeing jigsaw puzzles everywhere I went. I said, "Okay, Lord, okay." After a few "okay Lord, I hear You," He then started allowing emails and other visuals come to me about publishing. I finally stepped out on faith concerning professionally publishing. God can be funny at times.

During the editing process of this book, God showed me that the book was not complete, and it was a puzzle itself. I had to print out the manuscript; it was easier for me to find the mistakes. As I sat up in my bed for hours at a time making circles, rectangles, and other shapes on the manuscript, the Lord showed me how it looked like puzzle pieces I was assembling. I said all of that to say He already knew when this book would finally be released. He also knew that five years ago, I was not ready for the things that He has recently revealed to me that were added to this book.

Sometimes when we think we do not have a due date to finish

things, we really do. Everything has a due date, everything. It is all according to His divine timing.

Last Minute Producers

We tend to complain about the Lord not coming when we want Him to. At times we may feel like He moves too slow. But we have the audacity to lollygag around and wait until the last minute to do something for Him. And we expect Him to understand and even have the nerve to ask Him to help us when we feel like we are drowning trying to meet the deadline. Our gracious Father always seems to reach in and pull us out of our self-messes. Thank You, Lord. This is an ouch and amen for me.

Some of us will wait until the last minute to work on our assignment. And we wonder why we feel pressured at times. We may throw something together that we may think looks good. We will present it on the due date as if it were some of our best work. Some may not say it, but we can tell when something was thrown together at the last minute. It is normally sloppy, unorganized, and came straight from the flesh.

In a natural situation, if we were to have a job or school assignment due at a certain time, we would do whatever we need to do to get that assignment turned in on time. We would also make sure that the assignment is nice and presentable. Why is it when we do something for the Lord, we do not give Him the effort that we give for carnal people/things? When we represent Him, we should desire the spirit of excellence and for it to be solid. We must take our time and complete the assignment given to us.

Waiting until the last minute to produce something, anything could go wrong. The sabotage spirit is always alert, looking for a crack or crevice to slip right on in. By waiting until the last minute to work on something is like we are pretty much holding the door open for sabotage to step in. Know this: demonic spirits do not work alone. If we leave the door open for sabotage, it will bring the spirit of Boise to tamper with our electronics, anger, frustration, worry, and so on. *Imagine* how we allow unnecessary spirits in our midst to tamper with us because we may not feel like working on an assignment that we had a considerable time frame to complete.

Once, God showed me trying to hurry up and finish my homework at the last minute, and a dozen demons sitting around me trying to convince me to give up. Now, I can see why things feel more intense when waiting until the last minute to do something. Help us, Lord, not to procrastinate when we are given something to do, especially if it is for You, Lord. May we use Your time wisely by doing our best with the help of the spirit of excellence. In Jesus' name. Amen.

Aligning with His Divine Design

When we are not in alignment with His timing, it is like having a vehicle that is out of alignment. You know, when a vehicle runs into some things on the road, it may be knocked out of alignment. It may cause the steering wheel to be all shaky, pulling the car to the left or right. It may start to ruin the tires or something like that.

During my jigsaw puzzle assignment, God showed me that my obedience to Him was out of alignment. Once upon a time ago, I had no problem with obeying Him without having temper tantrums or questioning Him when He ordered me to do something for Him. I was once totally in "tune" with Him. This assignment was my tune-up. I needed to be realigned.

Think of it this way with me, please: We were placed on this earth to be vehicles for the Lord. We face so many trials and stumbling blocks along the way that may knock us out of alignment with God's divine plan He has for our life. When we are not aligned according to His divine design, things may appear to be shaky, pulling us in every direction. We may find it hard to move forward.

I am sure that at one point in our lives, we have felt like something was "off." We may not have known what it was, but we could feel it. Just as a car has a sensor to notify us when something is "off" with it, we have the Spirit of God nudging at us to let us know we need some maintenance work. We all need His fuel, the Word of God, to keep us going. We need fresh oil, fresh anointing, an alignment. I hear Him saying that many of us need a spiritual tune-up. Some may be in alignment with Him but need an oil change, fresh oil. Some may need fuel injector cleaner to unclog our engines from all the bad fuel we have been consuming. There is a lot of false doctrine being preached. If we intake it and try to live by it and realize that we are not moving, growing in Him, it may be because the bad fuel consumed was intended to be used as a stumbling block to slow down or stop us from spiritually growing. At one point or another, we all need a spiritual tune-up to make sure that we are in alignment-in tune with Him and His divine design. We all need maintenance from time to time. I hope this is blessing someone.

Aligning with His Timing

God is always on time because He is the Master Creator of time. He is Omniscient. He knows everything. When He created the heavens and earth, He also created the time that everything is revolved around. He knows exactly what second, minute, hour, day, week, month, year that something will happen. Time is a major part of His divine design.

It is not funny how we want God to move on our natural timing, but we do not want to align ourselves to His perfect timing because we feel at times, He moves too slow for us. We must always remember God is always on time. Time is His, and it is perfect. God designed the time from the beginning. He is the only One that knows when it will end. If we really believe that He is Omniscient, knowing every single thing, then we should know in order for Him to know it all, He had to create and design the precise time to insert in each part of His plan. Let us take a minute to think about how many times we have quoted, "He knows our end to our beginning" or "Nothing catches God by surprise." Do we really believe what we are saying? or is it just another cliché spoken? How is it that He knows every single strand of hair we have on our heads?

> *It is written*: "But even the very hairs of your head are all numbered" (Luke 12:7, KJV).

God's timing is so precise; when He designed it, He knew exactly what day, minute, even second that we would lose or grow a strand of hair. Come on, somebody, it is imperative to move precisely when He says move. We must be aligned to His time, not our own. He gave each of us our own individual time. We cannot expect God to revolve His plan around only our individual time.

Imagine this: You order food online through a delivery app. You expect the food to be at your door at a certain time, but you do not realize that when you placed the order, there was a series of processes the order has to go through before making it to your door. You place the order. The order makes it to the restaurant. The worker receives the order. Just because it made it to the restaurant does not mean the order has been picked up, been made packaged, gone from the kitchen to the front, been picked up by the delivery person, who might be caught in traffic, having car problems, or anything that can cause a delay. By the time the delivery person makes it to you, you are upset because the food did not come fast enough. Sometimes the delivery drivers have multiple orders and difficult drop-off locations. You do not understand that because you are at home, placed your order, paid for it, and want road runner services. That is selfish and unfair to everyone that has worked behind the scenes to get the order to you.

Same with the body of Christ. God has everything precisely timed, and if one of us falls out of line, it will throw the whole rhythm off. Bless the Lord that His body will never shut down. Glory to God. The message here is we need to stop expecting the Lord to reroute, stop or pause His design just to cater to us as individuals. We need to be on one accord working with other members, staying on track with His plan. Even trains have certain times to run. If a train ran when we think it is beneficial to us, there would be so many train crashes and derails.

Some Biblical Examples of Being in Alignment with God's Time:
Jesus and the Fig Tree (Matthew 21:19)

Earlier in the text, a demonstration was given about how Jesus cursed the fig tree that only bared leaves. That fig tree had a divine assignment to bear figs. It had an assignment to have produced figs on a certain day and time that Jesus was coming by. Jesus expected to feed on the tree, but it was fruitless. Jesus cursed the tree, and it immediately withered up. Just as Jesus had the power to tell that tree it would never bear another fig, He could have easily told it to produce figs right then and there. However, Jesus was demonstrating how important it is for everything that has breath to be in alignment with the Word of God and how imperative it is to be on His precise timing. When God designed everything in His plan, He had to put the time in its perspective places in order for everything to function and produce as it should. Many of us would say, "In a timely manner."

Elijah, the Ravens, and the Widow Woman
1 Kings 17:2-16 (KJV)

The Lord instructed Elijah to go to the east of the Cherith river to drink and had commanded the ravens to feed him there. The raven's assignment was to bring bread and meat to Elijah in the morning and in the evening. When the brooks dried up, God instructed Elijah to go to Zarephath where he would find a widow woman. He commanded to feed him. Elijah obeyed the Lord. He moved when the Lord told him to move. The ravens were in place at the right time, waiting on their assignment to show up. When he made it to Zarephath, the widow woman was right there at the right time gathering sticks. She did not know that she had been commanded to provide for Elijah; she thought she went to the gate of the city to gather sticks so she and her son could have their last meal. She had to line up with the word of God if she wanted to live. By the widow woman obeying the word of the prophet Elijah, they all ate continuously in the middle of a drought.

The Coin in the Fish's Mouth

Jesus instructed Peter to go down to the water and take a coin from out the first fish he caught mouth to pay their taxes with. In obedience to the Lord, Peter went down to the water and retrieved the coin from the fish's mouth.

> "Notwithstanding, lest we should offend them, go thou to the sea, and cast an hook, and take up the fish that first cometh up; and when thou hast opened his mouth, thou shalt find a piece of money: that take, and give unto them for Me and thee" (Matthew 17:27, KJV).

That fish that had the coin in his mouth had an assignment to be in that water, in the exact location Peter was in, at the exact time. Peter and the fish were both in alignment with God's timing which made it possible to produce a supernatural financial blessing causing Peter to pay the taxes for him and Jesus. If Peter had not moved when Jesus told him to, he would have missed the "money" fish. If the fish had not obeyed the Lord's assignment and not been in his designated location, he would have died with that coin in his mouth.

The Betrayal of Judas

It was a part of God's design for Judas to betray Jesus when he did. Judas did not have a choice in the matter. It was his assignment to betray Jesus. He already knew He would be betrayed by Judas.

It is written: "I speak not of you all: I know whom I have chosen: but that the scripture may be fulfilled, He that eateth bread with Me hath lifted up his heel against Me" (John 13:18, KJV).

Remember, Jesus instructed him to do what he had to do and do it quickly.

It is written: "And after the sop Satan entered into him. Then said Jesus unto him, That thou doest, do quickly" (John 13:27, KJV).

Time was of the essence. There was a set time for Satan to enter Judas and cause him to betray Jesus. After Judas betrayed Jesus, he felt so bothered that he committed suicide (Matthew 27:5). Judas did not know when Jesus chose him to be His disciple that his real assignment was to betray Jesus. It was an appointed time for the betrayal to manifest.

Job

God gave Satan a set time to inflict Job with sickness and sorrows. Job even confessed, "If a man die, shall he live again? All the days of my appointed time will I wait, till my change come" (Job 14:14, KJV). Job knew that he had an appointed time for his change to come.

When we are aligned with God's timing, it allows us to be in tune with the supernatural right here on earth. Some of us are too busy trying to do things in our own timing when we should realize that God is the one that gave us the time that we have, and we cannot keep deviating from His plan and His time.

Remember, a simple fig tree deviated from the plan and missed an important production time. As a result, it was cursed from the root. Again, the Lord said in Genesis 8:22, "Long as the earth remains there will be seed time and harvest." That means as long as every living thing is on the earth, we are supposed to be planting and producing. Our purpose is not to be sitting around doing nothing. We are on God's clock. If we are not productive, we are at risk of being cut off. Notice how we get so many warnings before something drastic happens? Truth be told, once we encounter the horrible situation, we may start to think about how we got into the situation. We think about what we should have, would have, could have done to prevent the situation from occurring.

Choose You This Day Whom You Will Serve

Choose You This Day Whom You Will Serve

Some of us will cry out to the Lord for help. He is gracious and merciful to forgive us, pick us up, dust us off, and place us back in good standing with Him, only for some of us to take His kindness for weakness and dive right back into the mess He rescued us from. God is not weak or stupid. God will not allow His children to control Him. He loves us, but we are going to reverently fear Him or be disciplined. We are not going to keep messing up His plans He already has designed for our lives. Since we have free will, we must make up our minds if we want to serve Him or not. We have a set time to do so. He will only allow so much grace for us. Again, we are not going to keep going against His plans and think He will keep allowing it.

> *It is written*: "Pride goeth before destruction, and an haughty spirit before a fall" (Proverbs 16:18, KJV).

> *It is written*: "He, that being often reproved hardeneth his neck, shall suddenly be destroyed, and that without remedy" (Proverbs 29:1, KJV).

If we love the Lord with everything in us, it will not be hard for us to submit to Him and move when He says move. How is it possible for us to love someone here on this earth so much to where we will do whatever they say, whenever they say, believe whatever they say? We can practically worship the ground that some of the people we love walk on, but when the Lord says obey, do this, or that, we have a problem with it. But we say we love Him.

We need to align ourselves with His Word, His design, His time. We need to reverently fear Him. Many of us do not fear the Lord. We disobey those we do not fear.

> God says, "The fear of the Lord is the beginning of wisdom: and the knowledge of the holy is understanding" (Proverbs 9:10, KJV).

> "And fear not them which kill the body but are not able to kill the soul: but rather fear Him which is able to destroy both soul and

body in hell" (Matthew 10:28, KJV).

If we reverently feared Him, we would line up with His Word. If we absolutely loved Him, we would obey Him. He does not want to hurt us. He said He knows the thoughts He has for us are good and not evil, but some of us are truly testing His patients with us. Some of us do not care how we are mistreating Him. Some of us are way out of line with Him, and He loves us so much to where He is allowing the confrontational ministers room to speak His heart with flint faces so we can get back in alignment with His design. Time is of the essence. God is not playing with us. So many of us are out of line with His time that is delaying other builder assignments.

When we look around at so many demonic things happening now, it appears that the demonic activities are more intense. The Lord says that there are prayer warriors off time, out of alignment. He says there are some people that are supposed to be over here, but they are too busy being hardheaded over there. He says many of the builders are slipping and sleeping. He says many builders are not fasting but eating far more than usual, causing us to feel tired and sleepy. Many of us are eating unhealthy foods. We are not nurturing our bodies as we should. He says many of us are playing sick to get attention from others. Many of us are on social media too much, watching too much television, working too many long hours, giving entirely too much of His time to worldly activities, and falling short with kingdom work. He says many of us that are doing kingdom work are being Martha's when He needs more Mary's. He says there are many of His people missing His divine time encounters because we are too busy caught up in our own ministries. We are too busy promoting our ministries and missing kingdom movements. The Lord is calling His kingdom builders to be realigned with His design. He has appointed times for everything, and we need to wait for those appointed times. We need to stop misusing His time that He gave us. His time is running low. We, as the body of Christ, need to line up with it quickly.

The Material/Supplies

"But my God shall supply all your need according to His riches in glory by Christ Jesus" (Philippians 4:19, KJV).

When we are given an assignment, we are also equipped with everything we need to fulfill the assignment. The Lord equips us with everything we need to complete whatever it is that He wants to be done. We must learn to wait on Him and trust Him. He always provides.

How many times have we quoted, "The Lord shall supply all my need according to His riches and glory by Christ Jesus"? Sometimes we quote scripture, and when the trials come to test us, some of us back up under pressure. I Am that I Am, sent me to remind His body that He does not lie. If He said it, then that settles it.

> *It is written*: "God is not a man, that He should lie; neither the son of man, that He should repent: hath He said, and shall He not do it? or hath He spoken, and shall He not make it good?" (Numbers 23:19, KJV).

We, as the body of Christ, have got to stop being double-minded when it comes down to doing things for the Lord. Either we are going to believe He supplies what we need, or we are not going to believe Him. We should not be wishy-washy about His Word. God is Jehovah Jireh. He is our provider. He is not going to tell us to go out and build something and not equip us with what we need to build. That is like sending construction workers to a construction site and telling them to build but do not give them the material to build with. Imagine that! Going out to a construction site with the instructions but no material; if the material is supplied for natural builders, then what makes us think that the Lord is not going to provide the material that we need to build for Him? *Selah!*

Telling on myself, when the Lord told me many years ago to write books, I was too busy focusing on how I was going to pay for having them published. He kept telling me to just write the books, and He will do the rest. In my mind, I could not see how it was going to happen, especially after researching how much it cost to publish a book. Over the years, God sent people to me to remind me to write. Many of the people I had never seen a day in my life. Many, I did know, but they did not know that I love writing. They did not know that the Lord had already spoken to me about writing books. Although I received the prophecies and assurances that it was God telling me to write the books, I was still trying to figure out how because my bank account was on life support. I had even thought at times to save the money I needed to publish, but something would always happen to not allow me to save money. I became a doubting Thomas. Especially after I published some poetry through a company that was more interested in me paying them to publish the work than to help get it in front of people. A few years later, I self-published a book of thoughts. The book ended up in the back of my closet. After that, from time to time, I would write but never finish the material. I just piled it on top of the closet with the rest of the unfinished manuscripts. More than fifteen years had passed, and I still had not published a book. Now here it is five more years later, totaling twenty years, I have finally decided to obey God no matter what it looks like. My bank account is still empty, but this time I refuse to allow money to stop me from doing something the Lord ordained me to do from the foundations of the world. It is by faith I am writing this book. I believe with all my heart that He has already provided everything needed to get this book out to His people. This is not my book, but His. I am just a willing vessel, finally. I hate that it had to take me twenty years to not worry about the resources as long as I am connected to the Main Source. In my mind, I thought I was late with finally obeying Him and completing this book, but God already knew when this book would be released. He had an appointed time. He knew when I would finally get in alignment for this divine assignment. Amen, thank You, Lord, for Your tender mercies in Jesus' name.

Wrong Ministry Motives

We, the body of Christ, desire to sit inside the walls of church houses and preach to our siblings that are already saved. Some of us get upset when our pastors do not allow us to preach. Many of us desire to be in the pulpit to be seen, and we will do just about anything to stand in the pulpit holding a microphone in our hands. We want everyone in the church to see us preach. We will make sure we invite all our family and friends to church on the days that we are preaching. Yet, we will not invite them to church when someone else is preaching. To tell the truth, half of the time, many of us will not attend church unless we are asked to minister or do something that would bring us recognition in church. When we minister, we will make sure that someone is sitting on the side to record us preaching. Many are not satisfied unless we are posting what we claim that we are doing for God on social media so everyone can see "us." We do all this preaching, and no one in the church feels any type of holy conviction to stop sinning. No one is offering salvation or prayer before ending the services, but we do not forget to ask for another offer. Some of our egos are so big that they overshadow humility. God is not getting the glory.

Many of the preachers today are more about "self" but cover it up by professing Jesus Christ. When I hear preachers in the pulpit saying, "I am going to preach," I will just lower my head and begin to pray. We are not supposed to go to church to hear the "I" preacher. We are supposed to attend church to hear what the Spirit of the Lord is saying through the preacher of that hour.

Also, we should not have to compete with one another trying to win our pastors' approval for us to stand in the pulpit to preach to individuals who are already saved. Jesus said, "The harvest is plentiful, but the laborers are few" (Matthew 9:37, KJV). There is plenty of kingdom work to do. Many of us do not want to go outside the walls and labor.

It is written: "And the lord said to the servant, Go out into the highways and hedges, and compel them to come in, that my house may be filled" (Luke 14:23, KJV).

Ministry is everywhere we go, not just the church houses. We, as the body of Christ, need to expand our minds. We need to put our hands to the plow. We need to get busy for the Lord and stop trying to find a way to profit/benefit from using His name.

Lying on God/Manipulating His People

The Lord says stop lying on Him. Stop using God's house as a den of thieves. Stop selling His prophecies. Stop having all these church fundraisers in His name and not using the funds to build His kingdom. Stop going to places telling people God said to give this or that. God says stop lying on Him. The Lord commanded us not to use His name in vain. He commanded us not to steal. He commanded us not to bear false witness/lie, but we (body of Christ) ignore, day in and year out, what He commanded. We take His love and kindness for a weakness. Yes, He is a forgiving, merciful, and gracious God, but how long do we think that He will keep showing mercy? We need to stop using His name in vain.

What is meant by that is we need to stop using His name to commit sin...get what we want. The body of Christ has it bad, lying on God to manipulate people into doing things for us. A good example is how some guest speakers at some churches will lift an offering, saying, "God said there are five of you that can sow a thousand-dollar seed." If one or two people come forth and sow, but no one else will, then the speaker will start badgering God's people for the money, saying they do not have faith in God, when really it is the speaker who has the lack of faith. If the speaker needed the money and trusted God, He could have easily touched one person's heart to contribute the amount of money needed with an overflow. Or if God would have said what was claimed to be said, He would have already placed it on the five people's hearts to give, and it should have been a confirmation. That is how God works. He is not a "just enough" God. He is The God of abundance, overflow. He is El Shaddai, our all-sufficient God! He is Jehovah Jireh, our provider! He is I Am that I Am, meaning He is everything we need and more.

The Lord compelled me to write this book. When I Am sends me in to "write" something, it is usually something "touchy that no one else will say" type of assignment He uses me for. I can feel the intensity as my hands type what is to be said.

The Mammon God

Many of us choose to sell kingdom knowledge that was given to us. Everyone may not have the financial ability to purchase the knowledge needed to effectively kingdom build. This is a huge problem in the body of Christ. There are more individuals in leadership that depend on the Mammon god to provide for "their" ministry than God Almighty. Could it be because these members know that the ministry was not given to them by God, but it was produced of their own free will? Again, if God ordained it, He would without a doubt sustain and maintain it.

To tell the truth, some of these ministries professing to be kingdom builders are charging ridiculous prices for tools to help other members successfully build. There are so many members in the body of Christ unable to effectively get the Lord's Word out because the teams that are attached to our assignments are taxing us on everything.

In this day and hour, church members do not want to labor for God for free, as it is called. Everybody wants to be paid for their labor. There is nothing wrong with being paid to labor, but we, as the body of Christ, are looking to the wrong individuals for payment. It is God who does the paying. He can use whomever He wants to use to pour financial blessings into our bosoms pressed down, shaken together, and running over, with good measure.

It is written: "Give, and it shall be given unto you; good measure, pressed down, and shaken together, and running over, shall men give into your bosom. For with the same measure that ye mete withal it shall be measured to you again" (Luke 6:38, KJV).

It is sad when we see individuals standing in a line at the church office waiting for a paycheck. Whatever happened to labor of love? Ushers on the door want a payment, the choir, musicians, cleaning crew, Sunday school teachers, everybody wants to get paid for their services.

I have been in church my whole life, have worked almost every position in the ministries and not one time has it ever crossed my mind to be paid for my labor. I loved serving for the Lord because I knew what I was doing was for Him. We, as the body of Christ, have got to get to that place in Him that we know that all that we do is for Him, and He will use others to bless us. We have got to stop looking at the church as just another business. We have got to stop jumping up going to church with one thing on our minds (getting paid).

I remember there was a time I hated going to church because it bothered me to see the offering being collected two and three times a service. The preacher would be watching the collection plate to see who was giving and who was not. Some would make members who did not have to give feel horrible.

Once, I stopped going to church, and my excuse was I did not have any money to put in the offering tray. I hated going to church and hearing about this social or that event going on, and all we had to pay was this or that amount. It would always be an amount I never had or could come up with.

Today churches are still like that. Some charge skyrocket registration fees. We will come up with a theme, design material for the theme, and tax those who attend, treating it as a natural event. Charging thirty and forty dollars for a five-dollar T-shirt, five-hundred dollars to sit in the VIP section and meet with the speaker afterward.

What about the members that are unable to pay the fees? How will these members be fed? Do we really think that God is telling us to do these things? I believe "a" god is speaking to these certain members. The name of that god is *Mammon*.

> *It is written*: "No one can serve two masters. Either you will hate the one and love the other, or you will be devoted to the one and despise the other. You cannot serve both God and money" (Matthew 6:24, NIV).

It is sad to see the Mammon god slip in and take ahold of so many members of the body of Christ.

> *It is also written*: "For the love of money is the root of all evil" (1 Timothy 6:10, KJV).

Please do not get it twisted. We do need money to operate the ministries. God does tell us to bring our first fruit tithes and offering to His house. It is sad how some of us are teaching the members that because the scripture is in the Old Testament, we do not have to abide by paying our tithes and offerings. If everyone were to pay tithes and offerings, as we should then, maybe there would not be so much error in the church concerning raising money to keep the doors open. Again, He equips us with everything we need.

Mammon Ministries Out of Line

He has already supplied everything needed for our divine assignments. He is just waiting on us to get in alignment with the assignment. If we are not in agreement with Him, how can we walk with Him? When we do not agree with Him, we are out of His divine alignment. When we are out of alignment, we cannot follow through with the assignment.

If we as the body of Christ are having difficulties with supplies and we know that the Lord has given us an assignment, we should not go out and attempt to make it happen on our own. Usually, when we try to go out and come up with the money or resources to follow through with God's plan, we are out of alignment.

By us being out of alignment, we may bring harm to other members in the body of Christ because some of us will lean to our own understanding and start charging ludicrous fees to the members to help raise the necessary finances needed for the assignment. We, as the body of Christ, are out of alignment somewhere; now we go in and knock other members out of alignment because the other members are trying to pay for the functions with money that is supposed to be used for other things.

Above all, we, as the body of Christ, are knocking the feeble and poverty-stricken members out of alignment and denying access to the Word of God because the members cannot pay the fees attached to the Word.

> *It is written*: "These twelve Jesus sent out with the following instructions: "Do not go among the Gentiles or enter any town of the Samaritans. Go rather to the lost sheep of Israel. As you go, proclaim this message: 'The kingdom of heaven has come near.' Heal the sick, raise the dead, cleanse those who have leprosy, [a] drive out demons. Freely you have received; freely give. Do not get any gold or silver or copper to take with you in your belts—no bag for the journey or extra shirt or sandals or a staff, for the worker is worth his keep" (Matthew 10:5-10, NIV).

Amplified Bible Classic Edition says:

> Jesus sent out these twelve, charging them, Go nowhere among the Gentiles and do not go into any town of the Samaritans; But go rather to the lost sheep of the house of Israel. And as you go, preach, saying, The kingdom of heaven is at hand! Cure the sick, raise the dead, cleanse the lepers, drive out demons. Freely (without pay) you have received, freely (without charge) give. Take no gold nor silver nor [even] copper money in your purses (belts); And do not take

a provision bag or a [a]wallet for a collection bag for your journey,
nor two undergarments, nor sandals, nor a staff; for the workman
deserves his support (his living, his food).

Matthew 10:5-10 (AMP)

Whoever started the idea of charging ridiculous fees for
church ministering functions could not have heard from the Lord.
The saddest thing is how it has infected the body of Christ and
spreading like wildfire. It is a disease, a disorder in the body of
Christ that needs to be purged. It is wrong to charge absurd fees
at a gathering that is declared to be called out by God, refusing the
opportunity of feeding *all* His sheep. Not one time did Jesus charge
for His preaching or any gathering He had. God always provided.
Charging for something that the Lord has already instructed that
we have freely received, and we are to freely give, is like slapping
Him in the face. He even instructed the disciples not to take money
from the people and to travel lightly.

When God sends some of us on assignments out of town or
wherever we expect the other members to pay for everything and
still go to the gathering and raise money to be remunerated for
preaching at the event. It is sad because the members that need to
hear the Word cannot afford to pay for the event. When God said
He supplies all our needs, He did not mean to turn His house into
a den of thieves. Many of us will sit up our little displays for the
members to purchase our material after a church gathering. Some
of us, as the body of Christ, take advantage by overcharging our
products. Some of the products are not even about lifting up the
name of the Lord. It is just an easy opportunity to make money
from the members of His body.

Some of us, sale clothing, make-up, hair, shoes, and so on in God's
house; we, as the body of Christ, are acting like the people that Jesus
had to flip the tables over on. Some of us go to church for profitable
gain. Prophets operating as psychics, sitting right in the house of God

with no shame charging His people for prophetic words. The Lord is not pleased with how some of us, as the body of Christ, have allowed the Mammon god to slip in the church house.

> *Again, it is written*: "No one can serve two masters. Either you will hate the one and love the other, or you will be devoted to the one and despise the other. You cannot serve both God and money" (Matthew 6:24, NIV).

Disobedient When Instructed by God to Give

There are some members the Lord speaks to concerning giving to the ministries and other members and do not obey Him when He says to give. We cannot out beat God giving. When He tells us to give to the ministry or a member, we need to put some action to it quickly. God cannot lie.

> *It is written*: "Give, and it will be given to you. A good measure, pressed down, shaken together and running over, will be poured into your lap. For with the measure you use, it will be measured to you" (Luke 6:38, NIV).

If we give a little, we will get back a little. If we give a lot, we will get back a lot. However, we must give what God purposed in our hearts to give. Sometimes it is seen in the church houses how some of us compete with one another when giving. Some members give a lot of money for us to have more leverage in the church. Sometimes we can tell who the big givers, small givers, and no givers are by the treatment shown to members by the pastors.

When I started this assignment years ago, the Lord gave me a vision of what His people, who He purposefully financially blessed to sow into ministry, were doing with His kingdom money. He allowed me to find the notes and instructed me to add them to this book.

Notes from Vision: Then

The Lord is showing me that there are some finances that need to be released in the natural, but there are some people that are holding them up because of their disobedience to His voice when He says to give. I can see women walking around with purses on their shoulders, and their shoulders slumped down because they are holding on to finances that they need to release. It may sound crazy, but how many of us know that God chooses the foolish things of the world to confound the wise? I see women struggling with big bags and walking with uneven shoulders in the spirit because the purses on their shoulders are too heavy. The bags they are dragging are like bricks. I see men's wallets in their back pockets, and I see women and other men's hands on their wallets. I see people at ATMs trying to make withdrawals, but their money is stuck. I see the devourer playing, swooshing through the neighborhoods, hanging at nail salons, bingo halls, gambling tables, and liquor stores.

I see the devourer on the internet stores hanging out and tempting people to spend. The devourer is at the restaurants, shopping malls, and car lots. He is everywhere, tempting God's people to spend their money frivolously. I see people not paying tithes. I see people not helping the widows and the needy, but they are helping the crooked people. They are sowing their money into devilish things that are ungodly. They are spending their money on fetish items. The more money that is made, the more it is spent on the twisted things of this world. Things that are "funky" to God's nostrils. For the love of money is the root of all evil. People have money to buy things to satisfy their flesh, but when it comes to giving to a good cause, you hear huffing and puffing and murmuring and complaining. Sometimes you do not hear anything at all.

The Afterthoughts: Then

It makes no sense how ministries are being held up because of financial lack. God has placed it on some members' hearts to sow into ministries and other members' lives, but we go on leaning to our own understanding and miss God because we did not obey when He told us to give. And we, as the body of Christ, wonder why we always find ourselves struggling financially more than we are financially successful. When some of us do obey and sow, we may put a limit on our sowing because of the amount of money we may have. Christians should have passed the level of the "twenty dollars" seed sowing. Twenty dollars is not enough money to build anything in the kingdom. Usually, when a believer blesses someone with twenty dollars, we normally go and buy something with it that will entertain the flesh, such as food, movie tickets, nails done, books, etc. Now do not get me wrong; there is nothing wrong with sowing that twenty-dollar seed. There are some members who may not have food or gas or no clean clothes, and the money may have served justice there.

What I am saying is we should not be so comfortable giving twenty dollars to a kingdom member and expect God to multiply our seed sown to twenty thousand dollars. If we want God to multiply our seed to larger amounts, we must sow larger amounts.

We (the body of Christ) must get past the thought "this church/preacher/ministry always asking for money" when they ask for money. Give, and it *shall* be given to us with good measure, pressed down, shaken together, and running over. We should not use the excuse that the preachers and ministries are crooked to keep from giving. Some ministries may be crooked, but we should not let it stop us from giving to other ministries. Everybody is not out to get our money and make us broke.

Most ministries are blessings. We sow into them, and we watch God grow our finances. We should not allow the behaviors of others to cause us to be scared to give. We are not scared to give money to buy three hundred-dollar shoes and purses. We are not scared to pay two and three thousand dollars for cruises. We are not scared to constantly spend money on that man/woman we will never marry. I am not throwing stones. I just would like for those who are scared to give to ministries to open their eyes and see the Word of God when it comes to giving. When we give sparingly, we will reap sparingly. When we give grudges, God is not pleased because God loves a *cheerful* giver. When we give cheerfully, it is a sign that we trust God will give back to us what we gave out and extra. We cannot beat God when it comes to giving.

> He said, "He that lends to the poor lends to the Lord and the Lord will repay" (Proverbs 19:17, KJV).

> Ecclesiastes 11:1 (KJV) says, "Cast thy bread upon the waters, for thou shalt find it after many days."

God's Word does *not* lie. We must stop leaning to our own understanding. We must stop being stingy and selfish when it comes to giving. If we are kingdom builders, we are supposed to work *together* to build. That even means if one of us does not have the finances for a ministry God has given us and another member does, it is that member's duty as a kingdom sibling in Christ to help with the ministry financially.

Remember how we lived in neighborhoods, and we all would look after one another's children? We were the village that raised the children. Today it is a dog-eat-dog world. People do not care anymore who is slacking as long as their hustle is flowing. No, the way things were back then when the neighbors helped raise their children was a natural demonstration of how it should be, spiritually. There are plenty of siblings in Christ that can help with ministries but choose not to because it is too many false ministries out here appearing real. That still does not give us the right to blow off kingdom finances. God does not bless us with tons of money to sow into the flesh or to give the devil satisfaction. He blesses us with finances to take care of the ministries, His ministries.

Some of us are quick to say we are not giving our money to certain preachers or ministries because they may not be as popular as the others, but we are quick to give all our money to these *mega* ministries that are not hurting for money and are more off into staying mega. They are not launching out. They are not making disciples, they are not casting out demons, they are not sheltering the homeless, but those are the ministries members of the body we prefer to sow all our money into. And we wonder why our finances are not increasing as they should.

It is something when a prophet comes to the church and asks us to sow a thousand-dollar seed. We will rush to our wallets and purses, write the check, overdraw our bank account, hock our jewelry, go half with another member to come up with those thousand dollars so we can go hear what prophecy he or she has for us. We are buying fortunes from a person operating as a wizard, warlock, witch. Anyone that knows the Word of God knows that *authentic* prophets/prophetesses come to blow the trumpet, to warn. At times God does allow a prophet to prophesy finances and prosperity for *free*. *True* prophets know that the words we speak are not our own words but God's, and it is *not* for sale. God said, *Freely you have been given, and freely you shall give.*

So, if we are paying for prophecies, we are in the midst of a wizard, warlock, witch, soothsayer, fortune teller, not a real prophet or prophetess. Sorry, but not sorry, we should know better. God is not honoring our seeds because they are being sown wrong. The same person that came up with the thousand-dollar seed to sow into the prophet had just sat up and told a homeless person a few hours earlier that they did not have a few dollars to buy them something to eat. It is sad to say, but it is a true error that needs to be corrected.

Now, do not get it twisted, the Word does say if you sow into a prophet, you shall receive a prophet's reward (Matthew 10:41), but I am sure that the Lord will place it on the heart of those He wants to sow into the prophet's lives. Remember, He has already placed it on the widow woman's heart to bless Elijah. Everybody cannot receive a prophet's reward. Many cannot handle it. The Lord did not tell us to go into churches and raise offerings for our ministries. True prophets should know that the Lord directly provides for us. Remember, the ravens fed Elijah every morning and night. The Lord does not want us walking around here begging for bread, especially when He has given it to us to tap into the supernatural and pull it into the natural. We walk around here preaching God; it is our source but milking the saints for all their bread, trying to pimp the anointing of God. Lord have mercy, please.

The body of Christ should not be lacking in anything. We have too many connections to be standing in need or cannot go forth because someone somewhere is sitting on the finances needed to maintain the ministries, and we do not want to give. That must stop in the name of Jesus. If we see someone in lack, especially a ministry, and we can help, by all means necessary, please help, and watch God bless with abundance. God will supernaturally stretch our finances and cause us to have an overflow. Or, if we choose not to give, God can blow on our money and cause it to scatter everywhere. I am so serious. How many times have we said, "I do not know where that money went; it looks like it just got away from me"? That is because we (the body of Christ) are not sowing it in the right places. That is how it is getting away from us.

Now with me, I never had a problem giving to people. My problem was giving to the church. To me, it was better to help the people standing in need because I got to choose who I wanted to help, but sometimes that was not always good because when you help people, sometimes some of them think you are their bank. They think that they come and withdraw every time they are in need. A friend of mine once said, "It is good to feed someone your fish, but it is better to teach them how to fish. Once they learn how to fish, they would not have to keep coming back to you to feed them fish".

This is one thing that helped me along the way with my giving. I do not hold back any information as to how to "get money" if I know of any way. But people these days want to charge you for information, or they want to keep the resources to themselves to keep the people "wrapped around their fingers" needing them. That is not God. Proverbs 21:26 (ESV) says, *"The righteous gives and does not hold back."* Why would we want to "hold back" information that will help someone else prosper in the kingdom? That is stinking thinking People are so scared that someone will have more than them or get ahead and no longer need their support, their help, so they would rather just sit up and watch them struggle. Or they will withhold the information just so the person that needs help must keep coming back to them and so they can have something to talk about. Oh, if any member in the body is doing this, better stop and repent, or you will be rewarded for it, but you will not like the reward you will get. That was for somebody for sure at this moment because my writing just shifted from one thing to something different. You better repent in Jesus' name if you want to be blessed. No matter what we sow, whether money, words, time, whatever, we will reap a harvest from it. We have got to be more careful about the seeds we sow.

The Builders/Workers

The Builders/Workers

Someone has a vision for a business. They write the vision down, and it is turned into a blueprint. They pick a location where they want the business to be. They handle all the necessary paperwork to legalize what they are going to build. They buy the property and pay for all the material needed to build up front. They hire every laborer needed to successfully build the design. They have all types of laborers in the midst of the project. They have beginner laborers, intermediate laborers, and skilled laborers. In the midst of the project, there are workers assigned to keeping the workplace clean. There are workers who are assigned to loading and unloading material. Some are assigned to handling the machines, heavy equipment; some are assigned to be security. Some are assigned as management. There are engineers, electricians, plumbers, welders, painters, roofers, carpenters. And there are the assigned builders. They all have different assignments but are all working together to manifest the vision on the blueprint.

In the midst of the assortments of contracted laborers, the beginner builders and workers have the potential and desire to build, but they need to be trained. They need structure and guidance. There are moderate builders who know how to build certain things but need the appropriate training to become a skilled laborer. There are skilled laborers that come in and working on specific things they have been trained to do. Some skilled workers may bring some special tools to work with them, but all the supplies they need to build with are already provided for by the ones the building belongs to.

We, the body of Christ, are all laborers. Everyone is not a *direct* builder, but everyone does have a part in the building process. We all have a job to do to complete the building. We are all not working on the exact same thing, but we are all working on *His* building.

> *It is written*: "For we are labourers together with God: ye are God's husbandry, ye are God's building" (1 Corinthians 3:9, KJV).

Some of us may have the same title and, working on the same things, but each individual skill makes the project special. When given the instructions to the assignment, all of our perceptions of it are different, which helps us to be originators, but at the same time still capable of comprehending how to work in unity to kingdom build for the Lord.

The laborers that have been assigned to directly build (like the natural laborers that work on assembling the building) are called the kingdom builders. We may hear kingdom movement, kingdom this, or kingdom that. And at the same time, we may be saying the other believers are behind. We are on a kingdom movement. Wrong, the other believers are working right with us building too. They just are not the direct builders. The members may be the cleaning crew, the ones that are assigned to keep the work area clean and safe from hazardous things that may cause a builder or other workers to stumble and fall. We have individuals in the body of Christ assigned to exposing and casting out devils. We have the skilled workers that come in using heavy equipment and bulldozing the false idols and gods of this world. The workers use heavy equipment to tear down religious works and the walls that the enemy has built in high places.

Imagine this: You have a class of kindergarten students, and you give them each a sheet of "construction" paper and a box of twelve count crayons. You tell them to draw a house with a window. Each child has received their "supplies" and "instructions" as what to build. They are all kindergarten students. Same title, but they all have different gifts (tools) and perceptions of the instruction that were given. Not one child in the class will draw the exact same picture. Even if they all use the same colors, their work will be different. Their work will be *originals*.

We are all originals; we cannot copy another member's gifts. No matter how hard we try, it will not be the same.

We are all one body, one Christ. Though it may be many members, we all have our specific assignment to do to build and to make the assignment a complete success. Some of us may carry the same titles, but that does not mean we have to compare ourselves to the other person with the same title.

> *It is written*: "Just as a body, though one, has many parts, but all its many parts form one body, so it is with Christ. For we were all baptized by[a] one Spirit so as to form one body—whether Jews or Gentiles, slave or free—and we were all given the one Spirit to drink. Even so the body is not made up of one part but of many. Now if the foot should say, "Because I am not a hand, I do not belong to the body," it would not for that reason stop being part of the body. And if the ear should say, "Because I am not an eye, I do not belong to the body," it would not for that reason stop being part of the body. If the whole body were an eye, where would the sense of hearing be? If the whole body were an ear, where would the sense of smell be? But in fact, God has placed the parts in the body, every one of them, just as He wanted them to be. If they were all one part, where would the body be? As it is, there are many parts, but one body. The eye cannot say to the hand, "I don't need you!" And the head cannot say to the feet, "I don't need you!" On the contrary, those parts of the body that seem to be weaker are indispensable, and the parts that we think are less honorable we treat with special honor. And the parts that are unpresentable are treated with special modesty, while our presentable parts need no special treatment. But God has put the body together, giving greater honor to the parts that lacked it, so that there should be no division in the body, but that its parts should have equal concern for each other. If one part suffers, every part suffers with it; if one part is honored, every part rejoices with it. Now you are the body of Christ, and each one of you is a part of it" (1 Corinthians 12:12-27, NIV).

We must be authentic and accept the gifts that God has given us alone and stop trying to duplicate the next person's gift. We need to stop feeling intimidated, envious, comparing, competing, hating one another because of what the next person is walking in. We are all unique in our own special way. We all need each other for the body to function as it was designed from the foundations of this world.

Imagine that you work at a construction site, and the foreman presents to you the blueprint of a building with the deadline to complete the building in five months. You are a skilled laborer, and you do not think about how much it cost to build it. You are more confident about meeting the deadline with other laborers working with you to complete the assignment. You have all the materials and heavy equipment you need to complete the assignment.

The Lord says He has given many of us assignments to complete, but we are too busy worried about the cost of the assignment. He has already paid for everything. Naturally, a construction worker heads to work daily with the expectancy that the supplies to build with are already there upon arrival. When they step on the construction site, their focus is on manifesting the blueprint's design effectively and completing the assignment on the contracted scheduled time.

We, as the body of Christ, need to stop worrying about the cost of ministry. If God gave it to us, He has already paid for it. We are the construction workers. Our job is to work on *the* assignment. Our job is to ensure that what we are building for the Lord is strong and sturdy. When He provides the finances for us to build with, we are not supposed to go out buying cheap, rinky-dink material that will make the whole project look dusty and cheap. When God supplies the finances for ministry, we are to use those finances wisely, but also in a way that when the spotlight is on the ministry, the people will see His glory. Let me clear the air a bit here.

Imagine this: God tells you to have a gathering at the church, and He wants purple, white, and gold decorations as a theme to emphasize royalty, holiness, and power. When the members He ordain to be at the gathering at that set time, He wants to show them something through the colors. He allows multiple resources to manifest for you to do as He instructs. However, you go and invite a big-time preacher from out of town to preach. You know it is going to be an awesome turnout because God showed you a vision of the glory. You think that inviting the brand name preacher to the gathering will draw in other members. You go through the motion booking the preacher, paying airfare, hotel fare and preacher fare, advertisement, and whatever other fees and fares. Then you see the money is looking funny. You go out to the little cheap stores and buy the decorations God told you to get for the services. Now you have sat up and spent God's money on material He did not instruct you to get.

That is like sending someone to the grocery store with a list of things to get, and you give them more than enough money to spend on the items on the list. But when they bring you the groceries, they only got a few things on the list but have spent your money on things they wanted to get instead.

Because you spent the kingdom finances on things other than what God had instructed, you turned His gathering into "your" gathering, stole from God. You did what you wanted to do with His money. God did not tell you to send for a *big-time* preacher. He was going to send forth an anointed mouthpiece from Him to your church to preach with power and demonstration. The preacher He was going to send was not going to charge you or the congregation money for preaching His Word. He was going to send in some souls that needed to be saved, healed, and delivered. But because you sent for the *big-time* preacher, you had to charge registration fees, entrance fees that the individuals He wanted to send in were not able to pay. Those souls could not get in the house because of the Mammon gods guarding the entrance. You had your gathering, and His glory was not even in the midst of you. The people only saw rinky-dink, cheap colors, and someone who was leaning to their own understanding put together a gathering on self-motives. The praise was not authentic.

It is written: "Unless the Lord builds the house, the builders labor in vain" (Psalm 127:1, NIV).

The parable was not written to condemn anyone; however, I do pray that it brought about a holy conviction to the heart of the reader that may be experiencing something similar to the parable and repent asking the Lord to change the error of the convicted members ways in Jesus' name we are to be good stewards over what God has given us.

> *It is written*: "There is therefore now no condemnation to them which are in Christ Jesus, who walk not after the flesh, but after the Spirit" (Romans 8:1, KJV).

> *It is written*: "Howbeit when He, the Spirit of truth, is come, He will guide you into all truth: for He shall not speak of Himself; but whatsoever He shall hear, that shall He speak: and He will shew you things to come" (John 16:13, KJV).

Big Time

We, as the body of Christ, need to stop running behind the big-time alleged ministries. Some of the ministries today are camouflaged devils imitating God's elect. Just because they have thousands of followers does not mean that they are followers of Jesus. Many of the "brand" named preachers and ministries are not sent from God Almighty. Some of these imposters in the headlines are itching ear motivational speakers. Some are employees for the Mammon god. There are some that were once called by God Almighty and that have gotten caught up in the fame and slipped out of being 100 percent uncompromising preacher of the Lord. It is so many unauthorized preachers that have risen and preaching a false doctrine of the Gospel. But because they sound good, look good, preaching what everyone wants to hear, twisting the Word of God, no one cares that God did not authorize them to preach. It is so easy to jump on social media, radio, and television now anything is slipping in, contaminating the Holy image of the body of Christ. It is too many churches and preachers in the headlines shaming God's name. There are wizards and warlocks in the pulpits, fortune tellers, soothsayers, professing to be prophets charging members of the body money in exchange for predicting their future. There are ATMs in the front and back of the church. The people are setting up tables in the church houses, selling things that do not promote the kingdom of God but their own "self" ministries. Most of these big-time preachers are sent in to oppress the children of God. Pressuring us to give to them the little that we have and promising that the Lord will bless us because we are sowing on good ground. Truth be told, the Lord will bless those who are unlearned or not able to discern the money-hungry bold wolves standing on a platform that supposedly belongs to God, manipulating the children of God to waste our kingdom finances on them to live frivolously with. Big preachers, fake anointing, hustling the children of God.

Imagine this: You are a parent in business with your son. You trust him and give him some money to invest in something beneficial for your business that would cause it to multiply. Later, you ask your son what he did with the money, and he tells you that someone said that they were your relative, and they told him they needed help fixing their car. They assured the son that you approved of him giving them the money and that they will pay him back double what they borrowed if he would help them. You later see that relative on social media flaunting, bragging about how many materialistic things they have. You even find out that person did not have a car. He did not represent anything he claimed to be.

How do we, as the body of Christ, think God feels when someone falsifies their identity to rip off His children? These people are lying on God to the children of God for financial gain. Our money is holy and has purpose. When we, as the body of Christ, manipulate someone for money and spend on our own fleshly desires, we are not taking from the people; we are taking from God. Kingdom robbing. *Selah!*

> It is written: "For there shall arise false christs and false prophets and shall show great signs and wonders, insomuch that, if it were possible, they shall deceive the very elect" (Matthew 24:24, KJV).

The Gear

> "Put on the whole armor of God that ye may be able to stand against the wiles of the devil for we wrestle not against flesh and blood, but against principalities, against powers, against the rulers of the darkness of this world, against spiritual wickedness in high places" (Ephesians 6:11-12, KJV).

Before a construction worker steps on the platform, they make sure they have all their safety equipment on and their special tools.

Construction workers wear safety goggles to protect their eyes from all the sawdust, dirt, and anything that may harm their vision; the Lord is saying while we are building to protect our eyes from the dirt of this world. Such as lust of the eye. The lust of the eye can cause us to fall into deadly sins. *Imagine* a construction worker that is not wearing eye protection. They may get some dirt in their eyes, causing them not to be able to see clearly. They will have to stop working to go and clean out their eyes so they can see clear enough to build. A construction worker is not going to build with dirt in their eyes. Same with us, when the lust of the eye distracts us, we stop building and focus on whatever has captured our sight. We must be careful of what we watch because whatever we watch will get in our spirit, and if it is not positive, it can corrupt our vision and poison our spirit.

Construction workers wear earplugs to protect their hearing. The Lord says to protect our ears from all the noises of the world. Stop listening to the "he said, she said" because we can become spiritually deaf if we allow people to constantly speak negativity in our ears. *Imagine* a construction worker going to work every day with no earplugs and hearing all the noise around them day in and day out. Somewhere down the line, the construction worker will find it difficult to hear because of constantly being around so many loud noises. Again, this is a great example of us as the body of Christ. If we continue to listen to the noise of the world and not protect our

147

ears, somewhere down the line, we will not be able to hear the voice of God because of all the noises of the world.

First which is natural, then which is spiritual (1 Corinthians 15:46). A construction worker must wear hard hats to protect their heads from any hard objects falling on them. The hard hats represent the helmet of salvation. He is saying to cover our own heads. He says, "Let this mind be in you that was also in Christ Jesus" (Philippians 2:5). He said for us to stop thinking like the world. Stop allowing the enemy to attack our minds. "A double-minded man is unstable in all his ways" (James 1:8). "We are a new creation in Christ; old things have passed away" (2 Corinthians 5:17). We, as the body of Christ, need to stop thinking about the old things. We are to cast down imaginations, and every high thing that exalts itself against the knowledge of God, and bringing into captivity every thought to the obedience of Christ (2 Corinthians 10:5). He is also saying we need to pray for our heads, our coverings, our leaders. Keep our mouths off them and cover them in prayer. He says stop giving those He has placed over us a hard time. Stop being rebellious when our leaders and/or those He has placed over us ask us to do things that will help promote the kingdom of God. Stop trying to usher authority over those whom He has placed over us. Stop having temper tantrums and quitting the ministry because the pastor will not allow us to have our own way. We are to honor our head, but do not, I repeat, do *not* worship our head/pastor. Only God is to be worshipped and praised. Amen.

Pastors must stop allowing the sheep/congregation to worship you. God is not pleased. He placed you over the sheep to look after and care for us. Not pimp or manipulate us or expect worship from us. Again, God is not pleased.

It is written: "Holy and Reverend is His name" (Psalm 111:9, KJV).

God says He has given us names, but we are using His name to gain worship from His children. The appointed time has come to clean up our work areas before He allows His cleaners to come in and clean it up, and we will not like it.

Construction workers wear special boots to protect themselves from stepping on sharp objects while on platforms. The Lord says to put on our spiritual boots to protect us from stepping on the sharp devices of the enemy. I see in the spirit traps laying before trails, and the people of God attempted to walk down the right path, but we are feeling pain, and we are turning and walking down dead-end roads because when we are trying to do right and walk straight and narrow, something is hindering us...something is causing us pain. I see spiritual knives and spikes on the roads. I see broken glass and nails planted on the roads. I can see members of the body turning around.

Satan, you have been exposed, and your booby traps will no longer work in the name of Jesus. People of God, we must put on our spiritual shoes, amen.

Construction workers wear tool belts, high visibility shirts or safety vests, gloves, and special clothing for whatever weather condition they are in. The Lord tells us to put on our whole armor of God, which consists of the belt of truth, breastplate of righteousness, shoes of peace, shield of faith, helmet of salvation, and the sword of the spirit, which is the Word of God. Again, first natural, and then spiritual. When we go on a natural job...construction site, we are going to make sure before we start working, we will have all the tools we need to protect ourselves while working. Before we leave the house, we must dress for work.

Same in the spirit, before leaving home, it is imperative to get up and get spiritually dressed for each day. If a construction worker is working on a bridge where vehicles are constantly passing by, they are going to make sure that they are wearing their high visibility vest to make sure they are seen by anyone operating in a vehicle. Just to think, if the construction worker is nonchalant about wearing their high visibility jacket to work just one day, they decide not to wear it...

and that one day will give the enemy a green light to come in and do what he does best.

It is vital to put on the *whole* armor of God. God says many of us are not putting it on and wonder why we are being attacked in our bodies. He says some of us attempt to put on the armor, but we pick and choose what we want to put on. For instance, some members have problems with lying and believing simple lies. Why? Because the member did not buckle up with that belt of truth. There are some members who have battles in the mind, being double-minded, allowing the enemy to speak freely to them, etc. Why? Because the member did not put the helmet of salvation on to be protected from wicked thoughts. The principalities, powers, the rulers of the darkness of this world, and spiritual wickedness in high places are lurking for individuals with little or no armor of God on. They cannot wait to attack.

I tell you the truth; I have a whole different revelation now about the importance of putting on your "whole" armor of God. He had to show me through construction building the importance of wearing that armor daily. When we do not put on our whole armor daily is like getting up going to work in undergarments only. We are setting ourselves up to go out and get hurt and may cause our co-workers to get hurt as well due to our lack of obeying orders.

Another thing the Lord shared with me about construction workers was one or two laborers cannot build a house or any kind of building alone. We have got to stop fighting one another when God brings us together to build. We have got to stop going to our little "leave me alone" corners and try to build on our own.

God's divine design was not created for us to work alone. Yes, prophets do walk alone, but God did not tell us to build alone. That is a big ouch and amen for me as well. We need to move "self" out of the way when it comes to building for God.

Construction workers are strong. There no disabled construction workers. We are all capable of doing the job God has assigned us to do. We need to get rid of the stinking thinking that tells us we cannot when God says we can. So, are we calling Him a liar?

Construction workers take risks every day they go to work. They know the dangers of their jobs. That is why they go in ready to take on anything ahead of them. We have got to stop fearing heights and depths. God is trying to take us higher and deeper in Him, but some of us do not want to leave the ground because we are afraid to go higher and deeper.

The first level of the building has already been built, and instead of going to the next level, some of us are sitting on the workbenches, saying, "I am not going up there; I might fall off." Do we really think that God will hire His laborers and let us fall...when we are working for Him? "Come up hither," says the Lord. We have got to stop being weak and backing out under pressure.

Construction workers know how to work in the heat, cold, rain, snow, etc. We, as children of God, need to be able to work under any condition. When the heat of the enemy is on, and even in the wilderness seasons, we need to know how to continue to work.

Construction workers work long hours, and they are hard laborers. Some of us do not want to put in the work in ministry. We may labor for a few hours and be ready to quit. Tell the truth. Personally, is the amount of laboring you do for the ministry right now and the type of laboring that you are doing, how would the building you are working on come out? Would the wolf be able to huff and puff and blow it down, or will God say, "Well done, My good and faithful servant"?

When construction workers are on the platform, you can tell they are at work. It is never quiet, and they are always busy. We have got to stay on the platform for the Lord and make some noise for Him. It is time out for the believers, sitting down and being quiet. Make some noise for the Lord. We need to let the devil know we are still working. We declare the rocks will not cry out because we are too quiet. The devil is a liar.

> *It is written*: "'I tell you,' He replied, 'if they keep quiet, the stones will cry out'" (Luke 19:40, NIV).

Construction workers know how to work together even when they have separate positions. The electrician comes in and does his part; the roofers do their part, etc. We have got to stop bashing our siblings in Christ about the part that God has given them to do. Just because He did not give it to this member does not mean He did not give it to the next member to do. I may be the one laying down the carpet, and another member may be the plumber, while someone else is the bricklayer. If a member was hired to lay the carpet, that member does have a special skill to do it. That member should not be trying to tell the plumber how to do their special skill. He knows what He is doing.

Again, the Lord has equipped each and every last one of us to do our special assignment. We should not single out individual workers and pick about how they are building as long as God is pleased. However, if some members are being stagnant, causing other members of the body to fall, our Boss will step in and demand correction; He may send other members out to speak warnings. Or He may send signs from all directions to catch our attention. He did say, "Pride goes before destruction, and a haughty spirit before a fall" (Proverbs 16:18, NIV). Pride will prevent us from seeing the errors of our ways. Pride will keep us from hearing the truth to help us change from wrongdoing.

We are to help each other build, not tear down what each other is building. There is only one person who has the power to order a demolition. I bind selfish, stubborn, leviathan, divination, Jezebel, Delilah, hindrance, slothfulness, procrastination be gone in the name of Jesus. Thank You, Lord, for hiring us and equipping us to build for Your glory and complete every assignment given to us without complications in Jesus's name. Amen.

The Construction Site

Sometimes we can pass by a construction site and see the *coming soon* sign. Then we pass by it a week or two later, and we see a work in process. We may pass by again a month later, and the building is up and open for business. There used to be once upon a time ago it would take months and almost years before the buildings were completed and ready to open for business. I have seen so many buildings put up overnight recently.

They did not waste any time. I often wonder about the businesses if a hurricane or tornado comes will it knock the building down. Another thought was, "Was it thrown up cheaply?" But the Lord spoke to me back in 2017, saying, "Some of the buildings that you see being built swiftly before your eyes represent My move. Some of My people are on the movement with Me. They mean business. They are working together in unity and following orders, obeying My Word, and doing as I say, and building. You may see the coming soon sign one day and look up and see new buildings the next. I move swiftly. And some of the buildings you see that are built swiftly that are not Me. They may build swiftly and be open

for business, but less than a year later, the business has been shut down, or it has turned into another business. They are signifying the imposters in the church. There are imitators of My Word. They are throwing up churches and ministries in My name to gain financially. Soon I will send in My winds to destroy them. I have not yet done so because some of My people are caught up in the crossfire of building with them. The wolves in sheep clothing have lured My children into these churches that I am not affiliated with, and they feed them lies and take all their money and live fat like a pig, but their time shall come. Their day of slaughter is near. I need you to go out and preach the true Gospel of Jesus Christ. I am going to place My anointing on you and send you into the feeble, desolate, and famished churches, and I want you to bring My children out. It is time for you to stop arguing and competing amongst each other about who is more powerful. The time is now; I need you to go and get My lost sheep," says the Lord.

God said to go get His sheep out of these sour and weak churches, these fake churches He is about to shut down. There are some members that are hungry for God. They want the truth. They are ready for the truth but keep going to the lying churches. The Lord says to go and gather His sheep. He will separate the wheat from the tare in Jesus' name.

There were times I saw buildings that had just been built, and then I look up three or five years later; they were being torn down and rebuilt. God showed me that some of our ministries look like they may be falling apart. God says, "Fret not; I am only rebuilding them to be bigger and better."

One day I was coming home from out of town, and I saw a house that looked like if you leaned on it, it would have gone crumbling down. It looked like it had not been lived in since the early 1900s. God showed me that He is about to blow on a lot of "man-made" ministries. They are condemned buildings in His eyes, and they are coming down.

A Hot Mess

Earlier I mentioned that when we look at a construction site, we see the picture of what is coming soon, but when we look over at the construction site, all we see is a big mess; what we see looks hardly anything like what the picture is showing. We may see piles of lumber or dirt on the site; we may hear loud noises and busy people. What we see may look like a "hot mess." We cannot imagine how such a pretty picture would come from all the trash and dirt around the site.

When it is all said and done, and the finishing touches are put on, the building is standing tall and beautiful.

When people see us on the outside, they may think we are a hot mess.

At one point or another in life, we may look in the mirror and see ourselves as a hot mess. That is when we must override what we see and speak what the Word of God says.

It is written: "For we walk by faith, not by sight" (2 Corinthians 5:7, KJV).

When we look in the mirror and try to cater to our "flawed" body (looks are deceiving God said...it is good), we will buff and buff up our flesh to make it look appealing to us and others, but it is not the flesh we are displeased with. It is what is on the inside of us that is leaking to the outside and making us think that we are not up to standards for ourselves and the world.

Personally, I hated looking in the mirror until one day, the Lord had me look deeper, and I saw the demons inside of me. The low self-esteem, spirit of depression, and doubt were holding the real me captive. I looked in the mirror and saw my skin flawed. It was dark, and I had rings around my eyes. My hair had fallen out in patches, and I could see a skeletal greyish-like being sucking the life out of me. I remember I once looked in the mirror like this before, and I saw the Holy Spirit in me, and it was beautiful. At that time, I was feeling confident and beautiful. I had lost that zeal slowly but surely because I was constantly being around people who were speaking negatively in my life. Making me think I was crazy, mean, a horrible person that nobody wanted to be around. I was a reject. I started believing what people were saying about me. I lost my zeal for God and picked up the low self-esteem, shame, doubt, weary, depressing spirits. When I looked in the mirror, all I could see were those spirits that were holding the real me captive. I was seeing a hot mess.

It does not matter how nice we try to dress, how much makeup we wear, or how much beauty sleep we get; if we are not feeling confident about what God says about us, deep down inside, there is a battle going. The real person inside is trying to be freed from the hot mess that is holding us bound.

Anytime we look in the mirror and are not satisfied with what we see, it may be that we are seeing something in us that should not be. Sometimes we may meet people on assignment to kill, steal, and destroy everything positive we think about ourselves. We may have unconsciously allowed them to sow rotten seeds in our lives. Later down the line, we may begin to look at ourselves deep within. Somewhere we may have slipped up and started to believe the lies spoken to us. Because we believed the lies and meditated on them, the poisonous seeds that were sown began to manifest in our lives, or maybe there is a root of bitterness we may have been carrying for someone, anger, sorrow, or despair...all of which are demonic seeds inside of us, and the more we hold on to them and keep hating someone, keep being bitter, keep feeling depressed, etc. Then guess what is happening? The seeds are growing inside of us. Sooner or later, they will manifest, leaking from the inside to the outside, making us feel insecure and unattractive. No makeup, haircut, trimmed beard, nice clothes, or cologne can cover up a foul demon.

The mirrors are there to show us the images we see of ourselves for the moment. If we do not like what we see in the mirror, then we should do something about it. And not by just working on our outward appearance. If we work on our inner self, it will leak onto the outer self. If we feel beautiful on the inside, it will show on the outside.

Remember that anytime we look in a mirror and do not like what we see, we should know that it is something demonic that is trying to weigh us down and keep the real person God created us to be from coming forward. Evict those evil spirits in Jesus' name. Do not let them fool you into thinking a fresh haircut, hair color, make-up, or whatever will make it go away. No sir, no ma'am. They are what they are. Demons can take over our bodies and try to keep us captivated. Again, if we are looking in the mirror and do not like what we see, chances are we are looking at something unhealthy, ungodly in us.

Getting Dirty

> "But the Lord said to Samuel, 'Do not consider his appearance or his height, for I have rejected him. The Lord does not look at the things people look at. People look at the outward appearance, but the Lord looks at the heart'" (1 Samuel 16:7, NIV).

Now, the same way people cannot see a nice picture coming from a heap of mess on a construction site, that is the same way with us, the body of Christ. People may see us as contaminated goods, broken, a hot mess, or worthless. What they fail to realize is that God is the Potter, and we are His clay. Long as we are in His hands, He can mold us to whatever He wants, and we will be perfect.

On a construction site, we may see a pile of dirt or a pile of rocks/bricks. God has shown me that a lot of His chosen vessels had dirty backgrounds. There may be things about us that other people know, and they try to make us feel like we are not worthy of being in good standings with God. I tell you the truth; I am so glad that God does not see us as the way others do. God looks at the heart while man looks at our sins, mainly our past sins.

God showed me how the pile of dirt is amongst a construction site for a purpose. How are we able to build without getting dirty? I do not know one construction worker/builder who works and does not get dirty. If you know of one, please let me know.

With the pile of bricks and/or rocks, God showed me on the construction sites how, in the process of building, so many people have stoned and wounded us. They tried and still try to keep us from building. God says the stone throwers' days are numbered. They need to think carefully about throwing stones at His property. If they damage anything that belongs to Him, they will have to pay for it. Let the truth be told: they cannot afford to pay for damaging His property. So, it is best not to throw stones. We have got to remember that God said, "Touch not My anointed and do My prophets no harm" (1 Chronicles 16:22, Psalm 105:15, KJV), and He meant just what He said.

Sometimes we touch people with our mouths. We may make mockery of what they are doing for God. Just because God did not give it to us does not mean He did not give it to them. Remember the story of Noah, how they mocked him for building a big boat on dry land. Those mockers died.

Also, know that after the construction workers finish building, everything is cleaned up; the mess that was made while building will be taken away afterward. The building will stand tall sparkling and new. However, it is still standing on top of the ground. No matter how solid the foundation is, dirt is still under it. I believe that God wants us to remember that no matter how tall we get in the kingdom on this earth, we are to still remember where we started from: the ground. We must always stay humble. We all have a dirty past. So please, if we as the body of Christ see our brother or sister in Christ getting "dirty" in their walk with Christ, let us pray for them.

If God leads us, we should restore them. Sometimes it is God's will for us to go through, for our anointing, but we must remember to not talk about one another while we are going through. Sometimes God will allow us to go through the same things our siblings are going through to teach us humility. No matter what we go through, we should always remember that we are all a part of God's body. We are still a part of the kingdom. We should pray for one another. We should not judge, least we be judged. We should never forget where we came from. We are never too clean to look down on someone else's dirt/sin. Jesus said it best, "He that is without sin, let him cast the first stone."

> *It is written*: "So when they continued asking Him, He lifted up Himself, and said unto them, He that is without sin among you, let him first cast a stone at her" (John 8:7, KJV).

Training in the Middle of Dirt

When construction workers build, they are in the middle of dirt, sawdust, heat, etc., and the more intense their job is, the dirtier they will get. We are builders for the kingdom of God. To be anointed workers, skilled laborers, before we can build effectively, we must know how to build. We must gain experience. We must go through a transformation. In our time of growing in the Lord, we fall, trip stumble. We go through our bloopers and blunders...and that is how we gain experience. No one said it would be easy, but our skills are much needed for the purpose. To be experienced, we must be taught. To be taught, we must go through something effective. Sometimes we can learn things and forget. That is because whatever that was, being taught was not effective. God will allow us to go through some things to gain experience and to make sure we do not forget what we have learned because somewhere down the line, we will have a pop quiz on what was taught. If we keep failing the test, we will have to take it over and over until the lesson is learned and the experience is gained. How many of us know that every time we re-test, the test is harder? It is wise to pay attention to every lesson learned. We must pay attention to the signs given and study to show ourselves approved. Experience does not come overnight. Amen.

> *It is written*: "Study to shew thyself approved unto God, a workman that needeth not to be ashamed, rightly dividing the word of truth" (2 Timothy 2:15, KJV).

> *It is written*: "And not only so, but we glory in tribulations also knowing that tribulation worketh patience; And patience, experience; and experience, hope: And hope maketh not ashamed;

because the love of God is shed abroad in our hearts by the Holy Ghost which is given unto us" (Romans 5:3-5, KJV).

Imagine this: You are hired to work as an employee at a fast-food restaurant. You have never worked on a job before, but you do have the knowledge of how to cook meat or make a sandwich. You do not know how to manage or run the restaurant. The hiring manager is not going to hire you as a manager that does not know anything about the fast-food business. However, they may see the potential. They will give you all the supplies you need to start. They will train you, show you how to use their special tools a little at a time. As time progresses, you are promoted to team leader. As a team leader, you are given more duties and responsibilities. You are learning more and more. You even notice how you are using good critical thinking skills and other things that the job could not teach you. As time progresses and you do too. You are finally promoted to the store manager, then to the area manager. With each promotion, you are equipped with what you need to successfully operate in your position.

Many of us think that we are supposed to jump right in and do things for the Lord. I remember when my pastor told me that I was a prophetess (I had no clue what a prophetess was, but I liked the sound of it), I went and told everybody I was a prophetess. The more I learned about the calling, I was saying, "Oh, I have been doing that since I was a child." I was saying things that would happen, and because I did not know about the prophetic, I was led to think I was psychic. I had some family members and classmates that had labeled me as a psychic. Everybody was cool with me being a "psychic," but when I came in the knowledge of the prophetic years later, as an adult, many despised and hated me. I could not understand how I was liked as a psychic but hated as a prophetess. After years and years of bloopers, blunders, bumping my head, being tried, and proved, I had learned that I did not need to announce to the world that I am God's prophetess. I also learned that just because

I was called and chosen by God to be His prophetic "courier," it was not an overnight thing. There were many times I wanted God to just kill me. I did not want to go through the making. It was too painful. To tell the truth, I am still growing, and any prophet or prophetess reading this with judging eyes thinks that have arrived; you are fooling yourself. God is always stretching us. It is not just the prophetic voices, but everyone that was chosen by the Lord to sit in any office or lead His sheep. We cannot become pastors, bishops, evangelists, apostles, teachers, prophets overnight. We are going to go through something, and we are going to grow through some things. Amen.

Biblical Example of Training in the Middle of Dirt: Exodus 2, Numbers 13

Moses was a deliverer. Before he was able to deliver the Israelites from out of the hands of pharaoh, God allowed Moses to be right in the midst of his enemy.

Moses had a front-row seat of how the enemy was oppressing God's people. God placed him in the same house of the man that sought out to kill him. Pharaoh raised him up, teaching him everything about the Egyptians lifestyle. Moses learned from his own enemy how to defeat him. How many of us know that God is the same yesterday, today, and forever? God will allow us to be right in the midst of the devil's turf for a season so that we can learn his tactics so that when we come out, we will know how to effectively go back in and rescue others who have fallen into the snares of the devil.

I would think it to be as we are undercover kingdom spies. Moses was a secret spy but did not know it at the time that the Lord placed him in the midst of his enemies to learn of them. Exodus 2 speaks of how Moses killed an Egyptian and hid him in the sand and later fled. Numbers 13 also mentions how the Lord told Moses to send men in to spy on the land of Canaan. When we hear the word "spy," some of us may think that it is an act of the devil, but truth be told,

God will allow us to be in the midst of dirt. It is in the midst of our mess when we are made. When God delivers us from that point of our lives, we know what it felt like; therefore, we should be humbled, loving, caring, understanding, and very anointed when we have to go back in to rescue our siblings that may be snared.

One thing about deliverance ministry, if we have not been through it ourselves, trying to minister to someone that is going through it may be ineffective because we really do not know what they may be experiencing at the time we are trying to help bring them out. Also, that could be dangerous to the individual who has not experienced the situation. They may not recognize the devil at work and may end up in the trap as well. We should never look down on someone that is going through their Egypt moments. Egypt moments are the things of the world that may appear to be fun but really is bondage.

When I was out on the streets doing everything wrong under the sun, I did not want to hear what a long dressed, Bible packing, holy rolly person who had not been a streetwalker, drug dealer, drug user, alcohol, gambling, whoremonger had to say. There was nothing they could tell me that would stick and make me consider coming off the streets. But when someone who was delivered from the streets and went through what I went through and knew the tricks of the enemy came back on the streets to tell me about a man named Jesus, I was able to hear, believe, and receive what they had to say because if Jesus did it for them, He could surely do it for me.

I was a "lost" builder for the kingdom of God. He allowed me to go through my seasons of frivolous and ruthless living so I would be able to come out and go back in and get the others that are going down the same road I was once traveling down.

I go back to the enemy camp to get my fallen brothers and sisters. That is one of the oldest tricks in the book where you step on your old stomping grounds, and the devil tries to remind you of your past bloopers and blunders when you are running on with the Lord. It was once said, "When the devil reminds you of your past, you remind him of his future." The only thing the devil is running is his mouth.

With that said, so what, because we have a past. Our past has passed. We are new creations in Christ, and those old things have passed away (2 Corinthians 5:17). If we stumble along the way, we have got to get up and dust that dirt off, repent, pick up our toolbelts and build. That dirt from our past God is going to use to get the glory out of us while we build for Him. God cleaned me up, but I am still radical and bold, but that is how He wants me to be for Him. When I was of the world, I kept a weapon on me and was always ready for war. Now it has flipped; I am radical and bold for the Lord, and I keep my weapon (the Word) with me all the time.

> *It is written*: "[f]or though the righteous fall seven times, they rise again, but the wicked stumble when calamity strikes" (Proverbs 24:16, NIV).

Whatever we went hard for in the world, God is going to flip it. We will have a strong desire to war against that tactic of the enemy as we are now in the Word. Who would have thought that all those hardcore fights I was having with men...I mean literally, blood battles, face disfiguring, body slamming, pistol-whipping, kidnapping, locking up in houses being held as a prisoner...all was training ground for me in the spirit realm. And guess what, that monkey went hard with me in the natural...I am going harder with him in the spirit. We are a force to be reckoned with. Someone help me tell the devil where to get off, please! He needs to recognize that we are not to be played with. God will take our dirt and our hurt and create masterpieces.

Remember, man came from the dirt of the ground, and God blew life in his nostrils. This part here is specifically for the member that is reading these words at this appointed time: do not ever let someone hold your "dirt" over your head again. Just remind them that builders got to get dirty. Buildings are built on top of dirt. If we see a clean builder, then we should know that they have not been working. Amen.

This reminds me of a time when I was small; I would hear females say they wanted a knight in shining armor to come and rescue them. I tell you the truth; I sure would not want a knight in shining armor because that shining armor signifies he does not know how to go to battle, or he has not been in a battle. Where is the soldier with the dirty armor? Where is the one that has been on the battlefield fighting for his people? That is the one we should look to. Unless we are queens, then we should not want a knight at all but a king. However, that is a different book, different story. Amen.

This book was not written to condemn anyone but to shine the light on some things that we as the body of Christ are doing that are causing the Church to be dysfunctional. We, as the body of Christ, need to stop being big babies. Stop being so offensive. Stop not wanting to hear the truth so we can keep living a lie. The Lord did not design His plan for us to be behaving like we are spiritually impaired.

The world is already full of hurting people. The last thing non-believers should be seeing is us, the body of Christ, hurting one another. They do not need to witness us acting like Pharisees. We need to be more like Christ, amen.

Trust when I say that every word spoken in this book, the Lord is holding me accountable for as well. Flesh knew it; that is why it did not want to come subject to His voice when I was given the assignment. The Lord said I was not going to speak His Word and think I would be excluded. There are a lot of things that have been revealed that do not personally pertain to me, but since I am a part of the body of Christ, I must adhere to these messages, be watchful and prayerful.

> "But I keep under my body and bring it into subjection: lest that by any means, when I have preached to others, I myself should be a castaway" (1 Corinthians 9:27, NIV).

164

Prayer

Father God, thank You for the opportunity to write this book by the guidance of the Holy Spirit. I ask that every soul that connects with this book at their appointed time read it with a softened heart, opened mind, and ears to hear Your voice through the words on every page in this book. I pray that this book is eye-opening and life-changing for readers around the globe. I pray that this book wakes up, shakes up, and stirs up Your body. May there be repentance, salvation, reconciliation revelation, interpretation, impartation, exhortation, rejuvenation, transformation, confirmation, and edification. May we be unified, and You, oh God, be magnified throughout the earth. May all the captives be freed in Jesus' name. Be glorified, Lord. Amen.

About the Author

Prophetic Courier is the Founder/Overseer of The Word's Organization and Proverbs 31: Women of Virtue International. Prophetic Courier is a transparent minister who loves to preach/teach God's unadulterated Word with power and demonstration. She has written, produced, and directed Christian Stage Plays such as *The Prodigal, In the Midst, The Devil Thought He Had Me, and Dearest Mama.*

CPSIA information can be obtained
at www.ICGtesting.com
Printed in the USA
BVHW061133080222
628386BV00012B/910

9 781637 697306